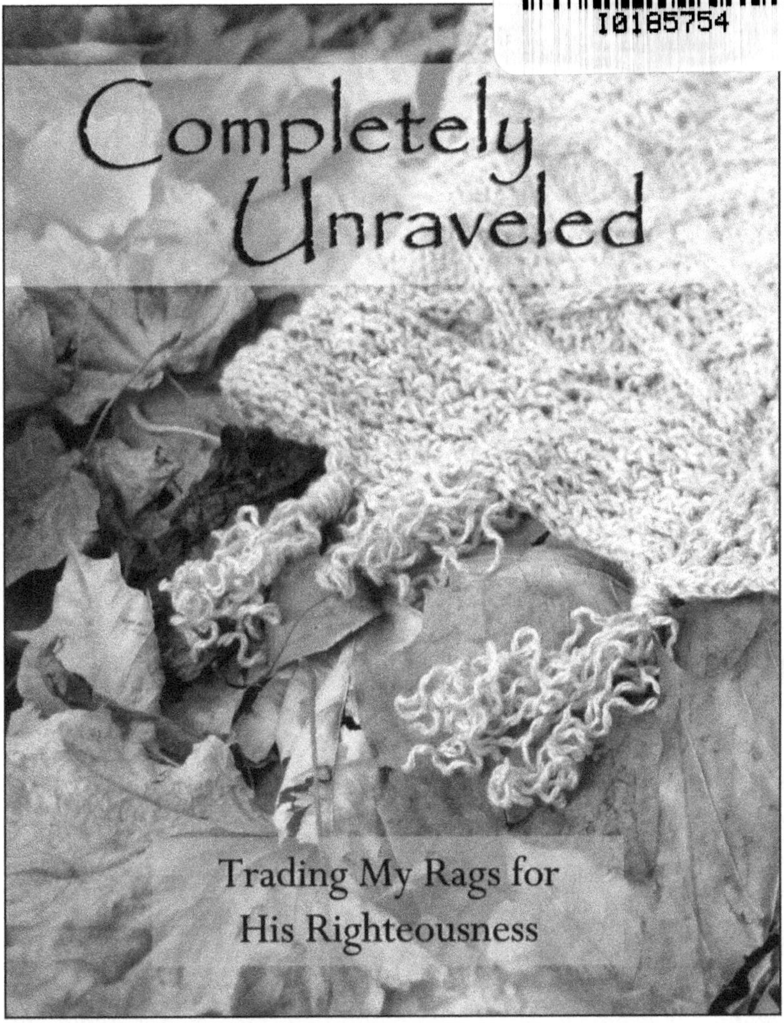

Completely Unraveled

Trading My Rags for His Righteousness

Nancy Dobies Duncan

Completely Unraveled
© 2015 by Nancy Dobies Duncan

This title is also available as an eBook. Visit
www.CreativeForcePress.com/titles for more information.

Published by Creative Force Press
4704 Pacific Ave, Suite C, Lacey, WA 98503
www.CreativeForcePress.com

Scriptures take from THE HOLY BIBLE, NEW INTERNATIONAL VERSION® NIV®
Copyright © 1973, 1978, 1984 by International Bible Society®
Used by permission. All rights reserved worldwide.

All rights reserved. No part of this publication may be reproduced, stored in a retrieval system, or transmitted in any form or by any means--for example, electronic, photocopy, recording--without the prior written permission of the publisher. Based on a true story. Names and locations may be changed. Scriptures quoted are taken from the

ISBN: 978-1-939989-23-9

Printed in the United States of America

My Prayer:

I waited patiently for the Lord;
He turned to me and heard my cry.
He lifted me out of the slimy pit,
Out of the mud and mire;
He set my feet on a rock,
And gave me a firm place to stand.
He put a new song in my mouth,
A hymn of praise to our God.
Many will see and fear and put their trust in their Lord.
— Psalms 40:1-4

"One of the things that is evident when I'm with Nancy is her utter dependence on God. She possesses a humility and deep gratitude toward God for being completely forgiven and healed from her past. Her gratefulness is always on the edge of her emotions when she speaks about God's love in her life, and that is why I believe she will be so powerful to minister healing to others." –D. McLain

Table of Contents

Preface: Growing Up	5
Introduction: Sharing My Heart	8
1 - Roots	10
2 - Family Matters	12
3 - Haze Gray and Under the Influence	23
4 - Hi, Wanna Get Married?	33
5 - Back on the Mainland	39
6 - Doby, Me and Baby Makes Three	43
7 - Broken Hearted	48
8 - Honorably Discharged	54
9 - Fences, Not Walls	58
10 - Don't Get in That Car!	67
11 - Accountability on Wheels	73
12 - Earlier Church Attempt	79
13 - My Son, Leo	81
14 - His Mysterious Ways	89
15 - Your Mission is Leo	94
16 - Band of Gypsies	99
17 - Unexpected Gifts	102
18 - Stretching, Feeling and Healing	106
19 - Rollercoaster Year	117
20 - He Hasn't Called	121
21 - Rags to Righteousness	125
22 - Sign Me Up	129
23 - The Switch Was Flipped	135
24 - Special Attention	138
25 - Leave a Message	143
Epilogue	152
Author Bio	161

Preface

Growing Up

"Truly I tell you, unless you change and become like little children, you will never enter the kingdom of heaven."
– Matthew 18:3

As a little girl I knew there was more – something besides what I could hear, see or touch. The white, flannel nightgown that had been a part of my Halloween costume the previous year was shorter now and hit my calves about midway. I didn't bother with getting the removable wings or halo. They were probably lost or broken by now anyway. Opening the door to the porch, I felt the warm, Santa Anna winds blowing; winds that come up from the southeast desert area of Southern California bringing unusually warm temperatures and are common in the fall months.

Sitting on the porch step, I laced my skates and crossed the grass excited to hit the sidewalk. The wind was blustering hard as I headed into it, pushing with all I had one skate in front of the other. I could feel the force, the power and the warmth on my face, blowing my nighty against my eight-year-old body. Two doors down, I turned around and decided to go in the direction the wind was blowing. Suddenly the natural push sent me sailing and I barely needed to skate. As the wind moved me along I imagined myself an angel floating forward. All at once I was lifted off the ground. For just a moment both skates and I were in the air. Not feet, not several inches, but enough to realize I was most definitely no longer in contact with the sidewalk. *Did that really happen?* It's a long ago memory and hard to believe, but at the time it was as real as the skates on my feet were. For that instant I flew.

At age five my family and I moved to California from Washington State. There were five of us kids and five bedrooms in the new house. My sisters being 5 and 10 years older than I each had their own room. My older brother had his own room too, since he was 9 and half years older than my younger brother. This being the case my younger brother and I shared a room until I was eleven. It wasn't until almost junior high when I had a room of my own.

Our twin beds on the linoleum floor had Peanuts characters on the bedspreads: Linus on my brother's and Lucy on mine. Linus was in his typical pose, holding his raggedy blue blanket and sucking his thumb. I often thought I ought to have the Linus bedspread because I sucked my finger and always had a piece of a blanket or nightgown with me. I did strange things with the silky edging part of the blanket. I'd rip it off and twist the end into a point and poke myself in the eye, up the nose, in my ear and other places. It wasn't until I was working as a CNA at a nursing home when one of the nurses dispensing medications in the dining room was talking to me about a foster child she took care of. This little girl would do the same thing with a piece of fabric. She said this was a form of masturbation. Those who have been abused sexually will often do this as a form of acting out. I had never heard this before and it made me wonder.

Sometimes the truth is right there in plain sight but the reality is just too much to handle. I tucked this information away for the time being. I wasn't actively seeking any answers at this point but it would make sense to me later while facing facts I'd not been able to before.

Introduction

Sharing My Heart

"Fear not, for I have redeemed you; I have summoned you by name; you are mine." – Isaiah 43:1b

This is not a story of revenge but of redemption and forgiveness. Even so I have found it difficult to write this important story. God has shown me it's time to communicate it but I have struggled with where I am at. *Am I ready to share what He wants me to share?* To know the Lord more and be in deeper relationship with Him is my heart's desire. I'm finding out that He is using this book writing project as part of the process of going deeper in Him. He is answering my prayer to know Him more intimately, to trust Him more.

I truly want to be the person he has created me to be and if it means bearing my soul and telling about myself and my life I will do so. In order to give Him the glory know that all my failures are my own and all my victories are because of Jesus. He has used both to bring about His purpose for my life which I believe is to help others be who God has called them to be. Despite my reservations, fears and insecurities, it would be worth everything if even one person would come to know Jesus Christ as their Lord and Savior and realize they too are here for a very special reason.

It is not that my upbringing was tragic or horrific. Actually it was probably typical of a lot of families. Maybe you'll connect to that: the ordinariness of it. Separating from a not-so-bad family is probably one of the biggest challenges but it's worth it to follow Christ and move in the direction He would have you move. I could have settled with the familiar (notice the word *family* in *famili*ar) but decided to move on with God. I've never regretted my decision. You won't either if you also decide to take hold of what God has for you. So with that in mind I set out to share my journey of how I've gone from rags to righteousness.

1

Roots

"For whatever is hidden is meant to be disclosed and whatever is concealed is meant to be brought into the open."
– Mark 4:22

When I began listening to Christian music on the radio in my early 30's, something wonderful happened: my defenses began to wear down. Listening and singing about Jesus and His love for humanity was heart breaking for me personally and my heart needed breaking. Over time it had become calloused and hard, covered with an impenetrable shield of self-preservation. My outlook on life had become quite cynical. When I began to actively seek emotional healing I saw how the negative experiences in my life and my reactions to them set me up for a destructive pattern; a sick and self-defeating pattern. Eventually through healing seminars and professional counseling, hidden resentment, bitterness and sometimes even rage was unearthed towards those closest to me. As I looked at events that happened to me as a child through an adult's eyes a new perspective slowly began to take the place of my jaundiced one.

As a believer in Jesus I say it is His grace and perfect timing that brought things to the surface. He knew exactly when I was able to face facts that had been suppressed so long. The desire to unravel the mystery of why I acted out in the way I had (heavy drinking, promiscuity and self-loathing) was the reason I kept searching my soul and my past to discover hidden wounds and get to the root of the issues. *Why do I react this way to certain things? Why have I made these poor choices?*

Most families prefer to keep secrets tucked away so tightly their existence is all but gone. If it wasn't for the secret's fallout that permeated my past (and my need to discover why) it may have remained buried like a corpse. *Something is festering. Something needs to be exhumed.*

Whatever it was that led me to begin a destructive pattern—a pattern that appeared before I was married, wreaked havoc in my first marriage and continued on even after that marriage ended—had to be unearthed. *Why do I feel worthless? Why am I incapable of intimacy? And, why do I always suspect there's something being kept from me?*

2

Family Matters

"Still another said, 'I will follow you, Lord, but first let me go back and say goodbye to my family.' Jesus replied, 'No one who puts his hand to the plow and looks back is fit for service in the kingdom of God.'" – Luke 9:61-62

I actually accepted Christ into my heart at a Christian camp when I was 12. A girl there whose name I cannot remember befriended me. I have always avoided initiating most anything (especially something that may involve rejection) so I typically avoided finding friends. Her openness and warmth was new to me. She seemed to shine from the inside out. She had no pretenses. She was straight forward. "Do you want to hang out?" meant do you want to hang out? Not, "There's no one else available, so I guess I'm stuck with you", or, "Hey, you're better than nobody, do you want to hang out?" No, she was honestly interested in being my friend for no reason at all. At some point the camp counselors asked if we campers wanted to invite Jesus into our heart. *Yes. Yes, I do.* Later they announced that baptisms would take place in the lake. This was all well and good until the rumor surfaced that there were snakes in the lake. The fear spread like a California wildfire and alas, I did not get baptized. I did not seal the deal.

When I got home the warm glow of my new status as a believer in Jesus Christ began to fade. The church we attended must have had what I later came to understand as "Spirit-filled believers," but if they were there they did not associate with our family.

My own home lacked the comforting, peaceful atmosphere I'd experienced at camp. *What was missing here?* I couldn't tell you then what was missing and it wasn't until many years later when I had my own *white funeral* (as Oswald Chambers refers to it – see Romans 6:4) did I understand how an inside-out glow happens; the same glow my new camp friend had. It was the in-filling of the Holy Spirit and the nurturing of that precious gift through reading the Word, prayer, worship and fellowship with other Spirit-filled believers.

Our family attended church twice on Sundays and once on Wednesday evenings. My friend Renee who lived across the street would come with me to vacation Bible school most summers. She moved into our neighborhood during third grade and was a transplant from Hauppauge, New York. Her dad quickly divorced her mom for his secretary, making the Redford's the first divorced family on our block. In fact I didn't know of any other divorced family until a few years later. In 1969 divorce was still rare. Kids from divorced parents seemed to me to grow up much quicker. The girls I knew seemed to have a worldliness a lot of us two-parent kids did not. I suppose the harsh reality that *all is not right with the world* becomes real to those who feel the emptiness left by a departing parent. My friend Renee had a boyfriend in 7th grade she kept all through high school. She was and is still a dear friend.

Living across the street and constantly being over at her house I was privy to the goings on in her home. Raising three girls without a father is tough, plus the obvious pain inflicted when a husband leaves the marriage for another woman. I know her mom had a lot of lingering anger and frustration and Renee being in the middle seemed to take the brunt of it. Renee was pretty. I think both my brothers had a crush on her. One time my younger brother even 'borrowed' a garnet ring my dad had brought back from Japan for my mom. He offered it to Renee, but when she turned him down it was eventually returned to its rightful owner. I am sure my younger brother regretted taking it afterward, having to endure being reminded a couple thousand times of how *you don't take something that is not yours,* not even if you believe she (mom) never wore it anyways. It's still stealing!

On one occasion I took change from a little black coin purse I'd found in my older brother's room. It couldn't have been much more that a dollar's worth. When he realized the crime had been committed, he told our mother. She didn't make a big deal of it but I recall Richard in his best vindictive, condemning voice leaning over the dining room table and saying, "Shaaame on you, shaaame on you!" in front of everyone. I felt crushed at that moment. Yes, I admitted the guilt for taking coins that didn't belong to me but was it worth the damning scorn my brother was heaping my way? I had the sense that this was minor in comparison to infractions he had committed against me and it left me feeling as though the ridicule I was experiencing was unjust and misplaced. *He* was shaming *me*? At the time I didn't know why there was so much frustration, pain and confusion attached to that moment until many years later, nor the irony. I knew what he was doing by making me feel guilty was more wrong than my taking the change. I sensed if someone ought to feel guilty it ought to be him.

My childhood was not one wrought with brutality or physical violence. In fact there was a lot of laughter in our home. The main mode of communication was sarcasm. The thing with sarcasm is it is lost on small children. Years of exposure and training, however, enabled me to hone the razor sharp skills it takes to be extremely cutting…'slice and dice' you might say.

My parents both worked. Dad was an electrical engineer who never went to college but worked his way up the ladder in government service for the Department of the Navy. Mom worked at JC Penney. She eventually retired after being employed by them for 30 years. She went to work after we ate dinner. My dad always drove her to the store 20 miles away and picked her up. My line when she arrived home was always the same, "What'd you get me?" Occasionally she brought home clothing that was marked down. I was always excited to get anything from my mom.

We were not poor – we were very middle class as most of the families in our suburban neighborhood were. Many of the dad's worked at either one or the other of the two Navy bases located a half hour from our town.

My friend, Penny, who I'd met during kindergarten lived around the corner and up the street. My mom asked her where she lived. She held up her hand using her two fingers to make a sign for little and said, "I live in a little bitty house," and again with the fingers spaced slightly further apart, "about this far away." There were periods of time in elementary school where I was no longer invited to hang out with Renee or Penny. Renee found a new neighbor, Debbie G, more interesting than I during third grade. Penny avoided me for the more popular Brenda Bytheway gang in fifth and sixth grades. By junior high we were hanging out again, all of us, but I knew it could change in an instant if someone else came along that didn't think I was cool enough to associate with. So I became more guarded.

My dad put in for a job transfer and got it, so at the beginning of my eighth grade year we moved to Long Island, New York. Having lived in California since age five the transition was difficult. I think the language barrier was especially trying. My math teacher spoke two foreign languages: algebra and *Lou-ong Oui-lind New Youww-kin*. Not only was math hard in itself but deciphering the accent made it even more challenging! Needless to say I did not do well in algebra...

The culture in our small town of Farmingville also lent itself to some interesting aspects of social interaction. The neighbor girl who lived across the street was a grade behind me and was one of six children. She had one older brother and one younger brother like me but that is where the similarities ended. I also met other girls in my classes and began to spend time with a couple of them who'd befriended me thus spending less time with my neighbor friend. This, as I came to understand it is reason enough to be *called out*.

When the doorbell rang one afternoon I opened the door to find the neighbor girl and her younger brother standing there: him wearing his black leather jacket, hands on his hips, and her pulling her gum at one end and twisting it and sticking it back in her mouth. Their posture said something was wrong and come to find out it was me. Unbeknownst to me once you make a friend in Farmingville you aren't allowed to have any others. I did not know this. "I'm coo-walling you out." I said, "What?" She repeated it in her Long Island accent, "I'm coo-walling you out!" "What?" She says, "Step outside." Apparently that's another way of saying *come here and let me beat you up*. I said, "No!" and shut the door on the both of them. *Great*.

It was the longest nine months I have ever spent anywhere. Perhaps if I was more extroverted, outgoing, easygoing or if I wasn't growing an inch a month or starting puberty it may have been more bearable. Needless to say, I was glad when my dad transferred back to the same job he'd left in California. We even moved back to the same town, only on the other side of it. I'd be close to the friends I'd left behind, sort of, but not close enough. It was a different school district, making it so I'd have to meet and make a whole new set of friends. *Great*.

I'd suddenly gone from 5'-1" to 5'-9" in the time we moved to and from New York. I hadn't seen one of my sisters in nine months. Shortly after we arrived in New York she turned 18 and wanted to move back to California. My folks bought her a one-way ticket based on the story she would be living with a *girlfriend* and looking for a job to support herself. So as I descended the stairs from the plane to the tarmac wearing red suede shoes with three inch wedges, making me an even 6 feet, she later said she barely recognized me. My height skyrocketed but my weight couldn't keep up. I weighed maybe 98 pounds.

Considering my new stature (yet same weight), after starting my freshman year at my new high school I was given the name 'Stick Woman.' A sophomore named Karen had been called that the year before, and she was delighted to have had the moniker removed and stuck on some new skinny girl. Most of the people didn't know or care that my *real* name was Nancy. "Stick woman got a cigarette? Stick woman can I bum a smoke? Stick woman got a light?" and so on. This name did nothing for my self-image as you might imagine. Boys could be friends but there would be no boyfriends.

Not that I was interested in any guy at school and even if I was, no one, I repeat *no one*, would ever know. In my first year of junior high I learned the lesson that if you like someone, keep it to yourself. At the time I did like someone and became the target of disdain, being ambushed on my way home from school when I walked passed the cute boy's house. I don't know how this boy found out other than I might have told a friend in confidence, but obviously it wasn't kept. It got so bad that I had to find alternate routes home because the most direct way went right by his house.

He and another boy, who I knew from elementary school,

would load up with the ugly, white landscaping rocks, stand on his balcony and hurl them at me as I passed by. Walking on the opposite side of the street didn't prevent some of them from hitting me. I remember the flush of heat rising from embarrassment, turning my cheeks bright red the closer I'd get to his house; embarrassed because he knew I liked him and because he obviously didn't care for me. Plus not knowing if they'd be out there on the balcony or if I'd escape a pummeling made me anxious as well. Unfortunately my school locker was also right above his which made it difficult (if not impossible) to use. I carried my books around most of the year rather than endure steely stares and possible loogies in my hair.

Some say if a boy is mean to you he likes you. This was not the case. He didn't like me or the fact I thought he was cute. The stonings eventually stopped but the damage was done and the message solidified. *It is dangerous to let a boy know you're attracted to him. Period.*

During the summer between 9th and 10th grade I bugged my parents enough that they eventually contacted the school district and worked it out so I could attend school with my friends on the other side of town. No sooner than when I started my sophomore year at the school I wanted, did my dad put in for another transfer. Florida here we come. *Great.*

We moved to another new home in a nice neighborhood with a clubhouse, tennis courts, swimming pool and hiking trails. Nice amenities, but I can count the number of times I went to the pool on one hand. *Who cares about it.* I hated the fact we had to move again and this time was even harder. I had to ride the bus to and from school only until I got my car: a 1968 Opal Cadet with three on the floor and a steering wheel big enough to steer a bus.

That car was the answer to prayer. It allowed me to go. I liked to go *a lot*. I drove to school and then to my job and home again. Often I would get in and drive south out of town, cut up on a road that led to the interstate and double back by heading north. That was my routine and I did this often. The freedom of it was addicting, as were the cigarettes I'd started smoking regularly. I'd listen to the only eight track tape I owned over, and over, and over: Queen's album *We are the Champions.*

When I did hang out with a friend it was usually someone who was way more experienced than I when it came to boys. One friend had a long-term boyfriend that she'd recently broke up with. We'd party and she even stayed at our house for a couple weeks until my mom said she had to go home. She would come over in the evening only to leave to go hang out with her ex, and then come back to our house…at all hours of the night.

Another friend was completely guy crazy. One of her conquests was a married man in our neighborhood. She seemed to need to have sex. I think he was her first and then she had several more lovers. Her parents didn't seem to think it was anything to be concerned about.

I remember going to a professional soccer game with both of these girls. They ended up talking about how they'd had abortions. Not cavalierly, but as two acquaintances suddenly being drawn together by similar experiences. At that moment I felt they were more suited to hang out with each other than with me, as I was still a virgin. I managed to graduate from high school a virgin but set out to do something about this virginity predicament. That is what I saw it as.

3

Haze Gray and Under the Influence

*"You are not your own; you were bought at a price.
Therefore, honor God with your body."*
– 1 Corinthians 6:19-20

By this time I was drinking heavily and often. Drugs such as cocaine and Quaaludes were also things I started dabbling in. The fellow who introduced me to cocaine was disappointed when all it did was send me on an inexhaustible run of conversation rather than make me want to hop into bed with him. I was a virgin as you know and it was going to take something that knocked my inhibitions and defenses down not hype them up. That is where Quaaludes came in. The group I hung out with after high school was all older guys who'd grown up in the town I now lived in. I met them through my friend and her brother; the friend who'd broken up with her boyfriend. Her brother lived with two roommates, and each of them had four wheel drive pick-up trucks with lift kits that made them seem larger than life and very cool. I began hanging out at their little abode we referred to as 'the ghetto.' It was the place to drink and the place where I eventually tried drugs.

One night I'd gone with my friend's brother somewhere in his truck. We were drinking rum and cokes and he gave me half of a Quaalude. We ended up back at the ghetto. That is where I had my first kiss and lost my virginity all in one night. It was not a big deal to me. *It was done.* I finally joined the ranks of the majority of my friends. I didn't feel like a woman. In fact I didn't feel anything.

And so went all of the rest of my escapades. I had one night stand after one night stand. I would be drunk. I would not know the person and I didn't care to ever see them again. This was my reckless pattern. Amongst the turbulence I did have a couple of short relationships: one with a guy 3 years younger. I was 18 and he was 15, unbeknownst to me. Thinking about it now I could have be charged with statutory rape. He, like a few others, complained that I would just lie there while he was on top of me. *What else was I supposed to do?* It was important to me that someone wanted to do 'it' with me...but I had no idea I was supposed to do something, too.

Eventually after moving back to, yes, the same town in California, I got a job at Jack in the Box. I was hanging out with Penny and my old friends again. The cycle continued: go out, drink, maybe meet someone, leave my friends, sleep with him, never see him again, usually. There was one guy who I saw exclusively for about 2 months. He took me out to dinner once. When the check came he didn't have enough money to cover the cost and I'd blown my paycheck so we had to leave without paying the entire bill (and obviously left no tip). *Boy, this guy likes me.* Actually I think he did. We saw each other until it was time to head off to boot camp.

Oh yes, at one point my parents were so fed up with my shenanigans my dad said, "Hey, why don't you call a recruiter?!" I replied, "Hey, why don't *you*?" and he did. *Great.*

It was late summer of 1982. I enlisted in the Navy for six years: four years with a two year extension. You had to enlist for that long in order to go into the Data Processing rate. I had qualified by scoring high enough on my ASFAB test; a test you are required to take so that your aptitude can be determined. Six months went by before I left for a six-week boot camp in Florida, which started in February. Actually, February and March are ideal months to be there. Florida's summer heat and humidity levels can be unbearable. I'd had a taste of that during the three years I lived there during high school.

Boot camp was interesting, exhausting, demeaning (but only if you didn't do what you were supposed to do) and rewarding. They housed us in barracks three stories high made of cinder blocks. During inspections, and there were a lot of them, I'd fix my eyes on the mortar lines and imagine a cross. I didn't know God but I knew of Him. I prayed every time we had an inspection and never failed one. *This prayer stuff must work...* They took us to a non-denominational church service on Sunday mornings, and although I enjoyed a church service now and then they were not mandatory. I often chose to stay back at the barracks on Sundays and tidy up my A-B locker. Evidently it paid off, or those prayers did.

Taking young recruits and training the *whatever* out of them in order to create a cohesive group of 80 young women is tough. For them to be all able to "fall in" and march in formation to a cadence of *yer left, yer leh ye ef, your left your right, your right yer left*, takes someone special. Our Company Commander, otherwise known as our CC, was Petty Officer (P.O.) First Class Cerna. She stood all of four feet nine inches and had a face that said *you will listen and do what I say or else*. I was able to stay out of her way for the most part, however she'd scowl at me during inspections. I figured it was because she had to careen her head backward to look at me from head to toe.

There were only two times I received 'special' attention from her. One was when it had been a particularly hot day and my nose began to bleed as we were lined up. We always lined up just prior to leaving the barracks. My nose began to drip blood, then it began to flow, heavily. She noticed the blood and yelled, "Who's getting blood on my centerboard!?" "I am, Ma'am!" I replied. "Get in that head and quit bleeding on my centerboard!"

"Aye aye, Ma'am!" I replied while turning quickly, and off I went to the head. Someone else was tasked with cleaning up my blood. Upon arriving at boot camp we'd been thoroughly poked and prodded. They called it a physical but it was more like being corralled and led through individual stalls where someone examined one end...and then off to another stall where (I am assuming) a doctor inspected the other. Blood draws were taken as well. This being the case, P.O. First Class Cerna took it for granted that I had no blood-born diseases, hence allowing another recruit to clean up after me.

The other incident occurred during an inspection when we were supposed to fall in – instead I *fell out*. For several nights I had difficulty breathing which really affected my sleep. During an inspection I collapsed. My breathing was labored and in order to not show any concern, P.O. Cerna yelled at me to get up and get outside. I followed her orders and by the time I got outside and hit the stairs I started to cry, which in turn opened my airways and my breathing improved. She gave everyone a smoke break so not to show favoritism. Shortly after that I was sent to medical, two buildings down from our barracks. Because I was alone I had to double time (*run* in other words). This wasn't easy, still not being able to breathe and all, but I made it. I signed in and sat down. Still exhausted I promptly dozed off. Next thing I knew a third class petty officer, who to us recruits was like a god, was standing over me. "Give me your notebook, recruit." Startled awake I handed over my notebook. Every recruit wrote their plan of the day in their notebook and we were required to carry it at all times. If you misbehaved in any way, which falling asleep is considered, and were caught by a superior they would require you to hand it over so a 'street-mark' could be added to your book. Street-marks meant extra drilling at an undisclosed location with a bunch of other bad girls. *Who cares...*I was so tired, I couldn't even feel scared about the prospect of being drilled mercilessly.

When it was my turn to be seen the petty officer took my vitals and listened to my lungs. When she was through she handed back my notebook sans the street marks and apologized for being so snarky. Apparently the way my lungs sounded she thought I had pneumonia: a good excuse to fall asleep. I was given a pass that allowed me to walk to the hospital where they'd called ahead and made an appointment for me A.S.A.P. I enjoyed my stroll although I was a bit paranoid. *What if I don't find the right building? Ah ha...* I did find it and the doctor asked me if I enjoyed living. This was the fourth week of boot camp so I had to think about that awhile. *Hmmm, well, not so much lately.*

He went on to say I had a severe case of bronchitis and I would have to quit smoking, take antibiotics and get some rest. *Great.* Beside the impetigo that developed on my chin and one more trip to the infirmary the rest of my boot camp was relatively uneventful. I managed to be advanced meritoriously to Seaman Apprentice right out of boot camp. I think they do this for all sickly people who survive.

From boot camp I was sent directly to Data Processing "A" school in San Diego, California. Gone were the tight controls, company commanders and prison-like conditions. Strangely I appreciated that controlled environment. When I enlisted I envisioned it being like the *Gomer Pyle* show where a sergeant yells in your ear all the time, where there is no free time and you're always under the watchful eye of somebody. I needed that. I knew I was my own worst enemy and needed the strict environment in order to *not* do what I typically did. Unfortunately it was gone and I was left to my own devices.

There were probably 20 males to every female on base in San Diego. I soon found myself engaging in one night stands until a guy in my class took an interest in me. He was from Georgia and he joined the military to avoid jail time for some drug charges. As I understood it his father pulled some strings to keep him out of jail. I sort of dated this fellow until graduation from "A" school then he was sent to the USS Inchon out of Norfolk VA. I got assigned to a command in Washington DC.

When I arrived in DC I had three days until I had to check in to my command. I could have called them and checked in early but I didn't know that was even an option. I was so green and had never been away from home; never in a place where all my relational ties seemed to be broken. It was scary. I didn't venture out of the hotel and when I did call the command on the day I was supposed to check in, they sent a duty driver right away to pick me up. The duty driver was someone I had just attended "A" school with. She apparently checked in early off leave. It was just a short time after dropping me off at the barracks that she introduced me to some airman who lived in the barracks on the Air Force side of the building. She'd gathered from my behavior in San Diego that I'd be looking to hook up with someone so she went out and found someone for me. That is not how I operated but since he was there... *Great.*

Time passed and during the second year in DC I fell madly in love with a barracks watch sailor. Or, madly infatuated I should say. A lot of us female sailors were enthralled with him and he spread himself pretty thin. He had a car like the Knight Rider. He'd let me take it for a ride so that he could be entertaining someone else.

Eventually I moved off base into an apartment with a couple who were promptly busted on a urinalysis test and had to move back into the barracks. I was stuck with the whole

$500 rent payment as an E-3. Fortunately a new female sailor to the command was looking for an off-base living situation. She was the best roommate I have ever had, except eventually her boyfriend moved in and I wasn't interested in the new living arrangement. When our lease was up, I found another apartment with two other girls from my command. This apartment was in Fort Washington, Maryland.

One night I was home alone and I'd started my period. It had been a couple of months or so since I had it, but I never was very regular so I didn't think anything of it. But then the bleeding got worse and worse. Tampons did nothing to stop the flow and the cramping was unbearable. I sat on the toilet bleeding and cramping. There was blood and clots and more blood and more cramping. After several hours of this I called a friend to come get me and take me to the hospital. *There is so much blood.* I don't remember how long I had to wait in the emergency room. When they did see me they said they would have to give me a catheter. I mentioned the fact that I had a tampon in, and did they want me to take it out. The nurse said that wouldn't be necessary. This was late 1983…I was 22 years old yet didn't know my anatomy enough to know that the urethra and vagina are two different things. The tests they ran showed that I was pregnant and was having a miscarriage.

They set up an appointment for me to return to the clinic at the hospital to have a D and C procedure. Knowing that didn't bother me. Even now as I write this I still have no feelings attached to those moments. I don't think it's ever seemed real. My drinking seemed to escalate around this time.

4

Hi, Wanna Get Married?

"For this reason a man will leave his father and mother and be united to his wife and they will become one flesh."
– Genesis 2:24

A few months later a friend hosted a birthday party for her roommate who also was attached to our command. Her roommate was gay so the ratio of men to women was poor – very poor when you consider some of the men there were also gay and most of the women were, too. My friend and I decided to head to Virginia where a mutual friend lived. Before we left I asked the hostess if she had *anything*, meaning drugs. She gave me some prescription drugs, Percacet. I took them and off we went. When we arrived a tall, handsome guy was there that I only knew as an acquaintance. Doby was his name. Between the drugs and alcohol I was overly affectionate and got him alone. He was funny. He was different. *I really like him.* We kissed for what seemed like hours. This wasn't my usual M.O. but I was enjoying this; enjoying him. We talked and kissed and at some point in the evening decided to get married.

The next day two friends took me shopping for a wedding ensemble. When we entered a shoe store I began to feel violently ill. I asked to use a bathroom, not normally for customers, where I threw up and was left with a splitting headache. Some of the thrill about getting married was wearing off. I was sobering up and not sure of what I was doing. The day before the wedding was supposed to take place Doby showed up at my work and asked to talk to me. We went next door to the cafeteria. He said he didn't want to marry me...unless he loved me and he didn't know me. I was relieved...and suddenly hungry. I hadn't eaten in two days.

We began dating. He had to drive 60 miles from one side of Maryland through Virginia to get to the other side where I lived. Eventually I moved closer to him during the final months before we actually did get married. Shortly after that I transferred to Hawaii for three years. I had to choose between Rhoda, Spain, Naples, Italy and Oahu, Hawaii. I chose Hawaii for one reason: my new husband had been previously stationed in Naples and I saw his photo albums with pictures of him and Italian girls he met while stationed there. *Naples was not an option.* Plus I figured if he was going to find work it would be easier in an English speaking country. Hawaii fit the bill for the most part.

Once we arrived on the sunny shores the partying continued. I wanted a different life style but didn't know how to change. *What would a different lifestyle even look like?* Not to mention our sex life had ground to an almost screeching halt after we said "I do." I found it difficult to have sex with my husband now that it was legal. I didn't know why. Shortly after renting our first place in Pearl City my husband asked me in frustration, "Why don't you ever initiate sex?" I literally found it impossible to do so. It was paralyzing. Before I'd always needed a drink or two before sex but now I *had* to be loaded to be intimate with him.

Our sex life was dismal. I wanted a baby and that was the only reason I wanted to have sex. After three years of marriage and no pregnancy I thought there had to be something wrong with one of us. We ended up going to the fertility clinic at Tripler Army Hospital. They took a sample of my uterus and a semen sample from my husband. Tests were inconclusive and they prescribed Clomed: a fertility drug. I had heard that multiple births were not uncommon with women who took this drug. Since I was due to transfer in June, I figured I'd take it in May so I wouldn't be very pregnant when I moved. Well, surprise! I was pregnant by March. Letting go of the stress associated with trying to make a baby contributed to making a baby! Also having sex more than once every two months increased the chances as well. *Silly me...*

When I transferred I was four months pregnant. *Now my new life style can finally begin.* Even prior to knowing I was carrying a baby I had cut out drinking. Before transferring, however, we went on a bike trip to the Big Island – not bicycles, but motorcycles (Harleys to be exact). My husband bought a 1984 Wide Glide in candy apple red. Friends from his first job in Hawaii were Harley owners. These new friends were Hawaiian locals who really took to my husband. They had a couple things in common: pot smoking and Harleys. Doby was also very outgoing and could make friends with a rock. Oddly, he decided not to go by "Doby," which is the only name I knew him as and went by his real first name, Christopher, or Chris for short to these new friends. This made me feel awkward when others addressed him that way. Anyway, they wanted to ride around the Big Island so three of us couples shipped our bikes over to Hawaii while we flew there. For three days we rode around the island with the local motorcycle club. We were told it was ran by a guy named Maitland. He wasn't thrilled with non-locals but since we were with two men who knew him personally we were accepted and allowed to ride with the club. I was feeling *different* and not in the mood to drink which is what most of them did after a day of riding. Eating and drinking were the laid back way of life. For some, smoking pot was, too.

My transfer date was June that year, 1988. My husband flew back to the mainland first. He was able to transfer to a post office in Waldorf, Maryland. While in Hawaii he'd been hired by the United States Postal Service by scoring an almost perfect score. On top of that his disability rating as a disabled vet added 10 points, boosting his score well over 100 percent. Even though this job provided a huge increase in income there always seemed to be friction between management and the regular workers. Doby often complained about this issue and transferred once from one P.O. to another while we were in Hawaii.

On the day he flew out a female co-worker was also there to say goodbye. She spent a good five minutes talking to him, alone. She was crying as she was hugging him and saying goodbye. I felt a bit out of place. *Uh, hmm...* I didn't even cry when he left. I didn't hug him as long either. I never thought about this being odd until years later, around 1997 when I was refinancing a home. My credit report showed that he had a P.O. Box unbeknownst to me at the post office he'd worked at in Waldorf, MD. When I saw that I instantly thought about the co-worker who had given him a long, tearful hug that day at the airport.

Once he arrived back on the mainland he stayed with friends in Virginia. He was commuting 50 miles one way to his new job in Waldorf. When I arrived we started to look for a house. Our plan was to buy a home rather than rent or live on base. His pot smoking influenced our decision to live off base.

I was supposed to be assigned to the Pentagon but told them

I had to decline the orders. The distance issue with my husband's work and the commute would have been too difficult. Also during my interview it was made clear I would have to undergo a polygraph test for the type of clearance needed to fill this particular billet (position). There was no way I could do that. If they asked about drug use (either mine or my husband's) I'd have to answer truthfully which could jeopardize my security clearance and even my career. I ended up with orders to DIA instead, the Defense Intelligence Agency, a joint service command located on Bolling Air Force Base. I was back on the mainland and back at the same base I lived at (in the barracks) my first year in the Navy.

5

Back on the Mainland

"...casting all your anxiety on Him, for He cares for you."
– 1 Peter 5:7

While at DIA I had the opportunity to listen to Admiral Boorda, the Chief of Naval Operations. He was a former enlisted man who worked his way up to the rank of Admiral. I found him to be humble and humorous. He told a story of his wife doing his laundry and turning his tee-shirts yellow and having to report for duty with one on under his whites (summer uniform). He was congenial and made us all feel at ease. Later I heard he killed himself after it was revealed that he claimed to have earned a particular honor that in fact he had not. I was shocked and saddened that he would take his own life for what seemed to be a minor infraction. But to a man of honor it was too much to bear. The disgrace of having lied about receiving something that other sailors earned by displaying their valor and courage was too much. Too much shame. What a pity. What a loss.

The friends we were staying with had a son and were planning their wedding. Our home search was taking longer than we expected and our presence made it more stressful. It was a very tense atmosphere. We were still at their home on their wedding day and the reception was being held in their backyard. My husband was the best man. He sat at the bridal party table, but not me. I felt like the odd man out at the reception. I didn't know a lot of people there and my husband was busy visiting and toasting at the VIP table. I spoke to him once, telling him I was going inside to lay down. My very bad cold was making me feel horrible. He was probably relieved for obvious reasons: his very pregnant wife was a bore at a party. The last thing I wanted to do that day was party. Then to add to it, I didn't feel well at all.

While lying down it began to feel as though an elephant was sitting on my chest. Breathing became difficult and the next day wasn't any better. In the infirmary/sick hall at Bolling Air Force Base I was diagnosed with bronchitis and sent home with antibiotics, cough syrup and an inhaler. I began to feel a bit better, but the coughing never quite subsided. Nights were even worse.

We eventually found a house in a neighborhood in Fort Washington, MD. The stucco exterior reminded me of the home I grew up in in California. It had a second story and a daylight basement. There was a fountain in the middle of the front lawn bookended by two beautiful, ornamental maple leaf trees. We referred to the fountain as *the dancing waters*. It had a circular plastic wheel made up of red, yellow, orange, blue and green that rotated in front of a bright light, changing the color of the water as it turned. Doby's commute was slightly longer than mine but a whole lot closer than traveling from Arlington, VA.

My coughing continued. Eventually I couldn't lie flat anymore without coughing uncontrollably. At one point I stacked four pillows on my knees and would lean forward onto them in order to stop coughing so I could sleep. Three times I ended up at the emergency room, unable to breathe, where they administered breathing treatments that cleared my clogged bronchioles. Finally I was assigned to a Pulmunologist named Dr. Weber at Malcolm Grow Medical Center on Andrews Air Force Base – the same base the President's plane, Air Force One, is based.

They ran a battery of tests to see what I was allergic to but it showed nothing. It was determined I had asthma; actually, *stress-induced* asthma. Once I was put on a regime of medications to open my airways I finally began to breathe easier. Prednisone, a steroid that inhibits the immune response, i.e., coughing, was prescribed as well. Dr. Weber tried to taper me off this several times to no avail. Side effects are lovely things like getting a swollen, moon-shaped face, a veracious appetite and irritability. *Great.* I thought once I delivered it would all go away. That didn't happen.

During my pregnancy I was also diagnosed with gestational

diabetes. I was given a sheet that listed the types of food to avoid and the ones to eat. Having been tall and slim dieting was not something I'd tried. However this was different. My baby's health would be impacted so I began to eat healthier than I had in years. Because the food choices were so low in carbohydrates, in order to get the calories they thought I should have my food intake was massive. I was eating tons of food it seemed. This went along with the nesting phase I was entering. Domesticity had not ever been my strong suite but now I was just cooking up a storm! In the past, my husband had done most of the cooking. He enjoyed it and was very good at it. It was *my* kitchen, however.

6

Doby, Me and Baby Makes Three

"Why do you look at the speck of sawdust in your brother's eye and pay no attention to the plank in your own eye? How can you say to your brother, 'Let me take the speck out of your eye,' when all the time there is a plank in your own eye?" – Matthew 7:3-4

My younger brother had come to stay with us after a stint in jail. I couldn't stand the thought of him being behind bars. While we were still in Hawaii I'd told him he could come live with us and get a new start on a new life when he was released. He came in October. My dad had given him $2000 to buy a car. He spent the first month taking taxis to a bar he'd discovered 30 miles away. He met a girl and occasionally didn't come home. With half the money gone and no car or job we said he had to look for work. That was the whole idea, right? Find a car, a job and a place to live...then a productive life can begin.

We helped find a car for him. He never did find a job and when the money was running out he'd hang around like a dark cloud, complaining there *wasn't anything to do here.* I called our mom and told her I was sending him back. She said, "Wait, you don't want to do that." I said, "Oh, yes I do." I bought a duffle bag, stocked it with candy bars and toiletries and booked a flight for Dec 7th out of Baltimore Washington International.

We dropped him off and said goodbye. The next day feeling not quite right, I called in sick. Being nine months pregnant they allowed me to forgo the formality of getting a formal sick leave approval. I took a shower and noticed a cool stream running down my legs. I assumed my water broke and called Doby. Because contractions hadn't begun yet I told him there was no reason to rush home. Even so, 15 minutes later he was at the house. We went to the hospital and while they were checking to see if my water broke a *woooshhh splaashhh* hit the stainless steel table then the hospital floor. If it wasn't broken already, it sure was now!

I had not dilated at all yet so they felt it necessary to induce my labor by giving me a drug called Pitocin. Contractions began soon thereafter and by 6:58 pm Leo James Dobles was born. Why do they say a *doctor* delivers the baby? Surely it is the mother who delivers the baby and the doctor simply receives it just like a quarter back delivers the football to a tight end or running back. The medical world truly has this terminology all backwards!

It was love at first sight. Well, almost. A photographer entered the room after I was reunited with my new son. Leo was in his bassinet sleeping. The photographer asked if I wanted pictures taken. "I don't think so," I said. After all, I'd just had this beautiful baby boy a few short hours ago, I hadn't slept very well and the stitches in my perinea area were starting to be very uncomfortable. *Time for some more Tylenol with codeine...* I politely turned down the opportunity for photos. It wasn't until days later when I wasn't taking any medication that I realized she was there to take pictures of my newborn, not me! *Oops...*

I truly did fall head over heels for my new baby. The feeling was something I'd never experienced before. It was more than warm fuzzies all over. Love took on a whole new meaning and it had nothing to do with what this little person could do for me. What was it? Attachment. There wasn't anyone else on the planet who I felt connected to like this – definitely not my mother or father, sisters or brothers, friends, not even my husband. I thought I knew what love was but I didn't. Not at all; not until now.

Once I got more comfortable with the idea I was responsible for this little life, my heart expanded. Yes I was a nervous wreck but it was worth all the anxiety. I now had my own 'always have to consider how your decisions are going to affect this child' child, and I loved it. Considering the emotional intensity and level of responsibility I don't know how people have more than one child. I really don't. Leo is my only child.

I had hoped my asthma would go away when I delivered like the gestational diabetes did but it didn't. Fatigue, lack of good sleep and not quite knowing what I was doing made me irritable, as did the steroids I took to keep me from coughing uncontrollably. *Breathing is helpful.* Leo was colicky in the evenings and often needed to be driven around in order for him to fall asleep. This was exhausting for both my husband and me. If only I had more confidence as a new mom. Some of my friends made motherhood seem effortless, but I was so afraid of somehow screwing up and causing something bad to happen. Looking back I wish I could have relaxed and enjoyed those first months. Maybe I wouldn't have expected so much from my husband either.

With my new found sobriety I was noticing that he drank often...daily. When a person has to have a beer-to-go camouflaged in a Coke can every time they get in the car, something's wrong. When he'd go to a friend's on the weekend and not be able to say no to shots of George Dickle, something's wrong. *Why do I have to be the responsible one all the time?* I had a tendency to focus on the negative and it was easier to accept that our problems were centered around Doby's drinking rather than look at myself and how I might be contributing to our mess. *How come he doesn't feel the same way about the baby as I do? Why won't he quit drinking like me, especially after Leo was born? How come when I want to discuss (yell) something he'd rather go out and have a beer and come home at God knows when, thinking everything is alright?*

The same ol' same ol' began to wear on me. I started to fantasize about the hardware rep at work. Not in a sexual way but in a *perhaps he likes me* sort of way. It was very immature of me and later I realized it was just a way to escape my feelings about my marriage and husband. Since I wasn't happy, I thought *why not separate*. And that's just what I did. I took Leo and moved about 2 miles away. My husband was distraught and didn't understand why. I don't blame him. I wasn't even sure of what I was doing or why.

He was a kind, caring, loving, funny guy who loved me and his son dearly and I was leaving him. Nearly every day we still visited him. I didn't want to deprive him of seeing Leo. He still wanted me but I couldn't see it. I was the vacillator who took the leaving part way too far. By this time however, he felt wounded and betrayed. He said, "You made your bed, now lie in it." Well, I figured that was it, even though he also said he couldn't live without me even after that. *It's too late now*. When I think about the ambivalence I had towards leaving him it astounds me. I didn't try to change. I didn't think I had a problem. In my mind it was all his fault. At the time I didn't know the meaning of "co-dependent" but that's exactly what I was.

7

Broken Hearted

"Do nothing out of selfish ambition or vain conceit, but in humility consider others better than yourselves."
– Philippians 2:3

I hadn't partied in a long time so one day I asked Doby if he would pick Leo up from childcare so I could hang out with some co-workers after work. We went for drinks at the club on base then to a park with swings and a teeter-totter. Soon afterward someone from the club came running and said, "Nancy, your husband called and he needs you to come home." Of course this was before the days of cell phones so I raced to the house not knowing what was wrong.

When I arrived Doby said his legs were so swollen he couldn't pull up his jeans. He didn't feel well and he was going to the emergency room. I took Leo home with me and waited. Soon hospital staff called and told me my husband was admitted to the hospital with congestive heart failure. As the person spoke those words out it seemed as though they were talking in slow motion. My mind could not register the news. I drove to the hospital, dumbfounded. While visiting my husband there I felt like an outsider. The gulf that had been growing between us suddenly turned into an ocean. More people came to visit and I stood holding Leo not saying anything. *What should I say?* It didn't seem real to me and I certainly didn't know how to decipher the seriousness of it all.

I visited him while he was in the hospital one more time. Since Leo had a cold I found a sitter to watch him so Doby wouldn't be exposed to his germs. While in ICU the nurse came in twice and said his heart monitor was indicating his heart function was all over the map. It was a short visit and I didn't stay long. He was released after ten days although his heart was only operating at 26 percent. I hadn't spoken with his doctor and didn't understand the severity of his situation.

For the next several days Doby slept downstairs on the main floor and I slept upstairs in our bedroom across from the nursery. On June 17th Leo had a pediatric appointment at Malcolm Grow Medical Center. He'd been really fussy and feverish. Tests showed his white blood cell count was extremely high indicating he was fighting a virus that would most likely run its course. The next day I awoke with pain in my ear. I went to Bolling Air Force base infirmary/sick hall. I was diagnosed with an ear infection and prescribed some antibiotics and drops for my ear. Later when I got home I fixed dinner and sat and talked to Doby awhile. I asked him if he'd like me to be syrupy sweet if I could. He said that I would have to attend a 'kiss your ass 101 class' if I wanted to be syrupy sweet, implying I didn't know how.

Shortly afterward, I went to lie down. My ear was hurting and I was exhausted from dealing with a sick baby the night before. Leo was contently hanging around his daddy's feet. No more than a few minutes after I went upstairs and started to drift off, I heard the loudest, most horrifying gasp gurgle coming from downstairs. I yelled, "Doby!" and flew down the stairs. He was sitting on the couch, eyes rolled back in his head. I pulled him off the couch by his feet and his 6'-4" frame slid to the floor. I grabbed the phone and dialed 911. After I told the operator what was happening she had me begin CPR. She was giving me instructions when my chin accidentally hung up the phone. Immediately I called right back and got the same operator. We picked up where we left off.

Sirens whirled in the distance, arriving a few minutes later. The EMT's took over performing CPR so I picked up the baby and was escorted into the kitchen. The ambulance crew began asking me questions while the paramedics attempted to use a defibrillator on Doby. I told the fellow asking me questions about his heart condition and medications. He had me and the baby get into one ambulance with him while Doby was taken by another ambulance to the hospital. I asked if they were able to revive him at all and he said yes.

He drove slow, taking a route I was unfamiliar with and we arrived after Doby had been taken inside the hospital. I was asked to call someone so I called Bryan, my husband's best friend. They waited until Bryan arrived to announce to both of us that he was dead. *Dead?* I was allowed to see him one more time. He had an apparatus in his mouth: the kind they use to connect to the balloon that squeezes air into a person's lungs. They encouraged me to touch him while he was still warm. I don't even remember if I did or not. By that time other friends had started arriving. I had to answer questions from a sheriff's deputy before I left probably to rule out foul play. I went home. Another friend who had arrived after hearing the news drove me. Those hours are all a blur...

Everyone wanted to know what happened and who knows how many times I told the story. I made sure to call his cardiologist, an Indian doctor who had his practice outside of the hospital, to let him know Doby had died. I asked him if it was always a possibility that he'd die or what. Apparently I didn't understand he was gravely ill. He asked me if we'd had an argument or sex before he died. "No," I said. After that I don't know what he said. It didn't matter.

Co-workers helped me when it came to the viewing. They brought food and served it. These ladies were angels to me. They were from Maryland and Virginia and they understood the importance of food when there's been a death. I didn't have to worry about a thing. They took care of it all. There were two viewings at my in-laws' request. The whole thing was very surreal and I was not quite sure how long I had to stay. My folks had gone back to the house after the first one. I didn't have a car so I asked my husband's Aunt Terry for a ride. I got in the back while my mother-in-law sat up front. As we got in my mother-in-law said, "She killed him," referring to me. Aunt Terry said, "Oh, no Patricia." I never quite understood my in-laws. I understood she was grieving now and I wasn't overly surprised by the comment. *I do feel responsible in a way. I left him.* Even though I saw him pretty much every day I must have broken his heart. He'd even said he couldn't live without me. Now he was dead. *Maybe she is right. I killed him or least was an accomplice.*

Doby was the youngest of her two boys and she adored him. He was funny and more of a people person than his older brother. They tolerated me, I guess. The fact that I wasn't Catholic was always a sore spot. I didn't know their son was Catholic. He didn't attend mass or practice any other aspects of the religion. That doesn't matter though, I found out: once a Catholic, always a Catholic according to the in-laws. When I was introduced to his parents and Doby announced we were getting married his mother fainted, sort of. So began a long and mostly awkward relationship. They tolerated me and I them. It was always clear to me that Mrs. Dobles thought I was not good enough for their son. My inferiority complex was fed even more by this knowledge. My insecurities grew after my relationship with them rather than subsiding.

Separating from him was motivated out of a desire for change. I was immature and thought my leaving would spur him to change. Unfortunately I wasn't aware the problems were *ours* not just *his*. At the time I fully believed his drinking was the root cause of all my unhappiness. *If only he didn't drink then everything would be better.* Since becoming a believer in Jesus Christ I have grown in my knowledge of who I am in Him. When I look back at who I used to be it's painfully evident that I had serious issues, unresolved anger, bitterness, buried hurts, etc., that needed healing; healing that only Jesus could perform. It would take several years before I could recognize how I was just as much to blame for our marriage woes. I didn't know what a healthy marriage looked like, let alone a holy one.

8

Honorably Discharged

"The Lord will keep you from all harm; he will watch over your life." – Psalm 121:7

I chose to get out of the Navy with a hardship discharge. In July of 1990 the trouble between Iraq and Kuwait began. By August U.S. military services were on alert. What was called Desert Shield did not escalate to Desert Storm (the war against Iraq to free Kuwait from Saddam Hussein's control) until January 15, 1991. However being widowed and sent off to war would require signing custodianship of my son over to someone while I was deployed. In a lot of cases it is the grandparents. I did not want to do this so getting discharged seemed the most logical thing to do.

I was honorably discharged in October of 1990. They say after a significant life trauma, i.e., death of spouse, do not make any big changes like quitting a job, moving, etc. I did both and didn't regret it (except later when it came to thinking about retirement and not having any). After 9/11 I tried to re-enlist. A sense of patriotic duty and the potential for retirement motivated me. I got all the way through the physical – even the part for those over 40 which included tests for glaucoma and other age-related conditions. Having had a history of asthma and being considered 10% disabled I had to undergo lung efficiency evaluations at the Navy hospital. Based on the findings of these tests (deficiencies in my lungs capacity) I wasn't allowed to re-enlist. It was a blessing in disguise. In March 2003 we invaded Iraq. At the time of the Iraq War nearly 220,000 reservists were on active duty. Had I been accepted the same issue of custodianship would have had to be decided again.

After being discharged in 1990 I moved to Washington State where my parents lived. I was hired by a government contractor and moved to the Kitsap Peninsula. My new job only lasted five months. Strangely I found it difficult to decide what to wear to work. Having worn a uniform for almost nine years made figuring out a work-appropriate outfit hard for me! Also a fellow at work took an interest in me. After turning down his lunch invitations a couple of times he asked me out in front of his boss. I felt awkward but didn't want him to look bad in front of his boss so I finally said yes. We walked off base to a place for lunch. On the way back I said something like *it's my turn to take you next time*. I felt I had to say something and that is what came out. *Shoot...I wish I could reel that back in*. I really had no intentions of seeing him again and definitely wasn't interested in dating him, or anyone for that matter. I hadn't even been widowed a year yet.

Well, he persisted in contacting me. My two co-workers were nice enough to tell him I'd gone or that I wasn't there. I didn't like having them lie but I just couldn't tell him myself. Eventually I quit my job due to the awkwardness and immediately started to look for another. That was May of 1991 and I didn't get hired again until December of that year. It was another contractor job at another military base. Eventually I quit that job to attend the local community college. I completed three quarters. School was tough. *Working is easier, plus I could use the income.*

I signed up for Certified Nurse's Aide training and was hired by the nursing home that trained me upon completion and passing the course. I worked on the heavy care unit until an employee tried to run me over with a patient's wheelchair...with the patient in it! There were complaints about our co-workers by other new employees, but since these co-workers were long term employee's the problems we were having fell on deaf years. I ended up quitting.

A few months later I received a call and was offered a position as a bath aid on the Alzheimer's unit. I met the person I'd be working with and said yes immediately. She was the most down to earth, straight-forward person and had a warm personality. Only problem was she was eight months pregnant and would be moving back to Michigan after she had the baby and her husband got out of the Navy.

Great.

My new partner was someone who'd worked there a long time. Bath aid hours were shorter than a regular aide's shift but it was easy to pick up extra hours. One thing that seems to be a given at nursing homes is always being short on employees. Very often employees were asked to work an extra shift...very often. That explained why our complaints hadn't gotten any results: ultra-dedicated employees were given a pass. My new partner was not as easy to work with as I'd hoped. I hadn't learned about boundaries yet and when she'd ask me about what I'd done over the weekend or what I thought about this or that I would give her a full data dump. I spilled it all: giving information about myself, my activities, my love life, etc. By now I was in a new *on again off again* relationship.

9

Fences, Not Walls

"Now the Lord is the Spirit, and where the Spirit of the Lord is, there is freedom." – 2 Corinthians 3:17

I stumbled on a book by Melody Beattie about relationship boundaries. I didn't know what they were. When I read that book a new world opened up. I even started experimenting with them, like when my bath aid partner would ask me something I would have previously gushed about. Instead I started giving short, yet courteous answers. It felt weird at first. *Am I being rude? Should I spill more information than I am?* But, then the strangest thing happened: I started feeling more, I guess the word would be *contained*. I wasn't all over the place in my emotions and thoughts. I was beginning to understand that I wasn't responsible for other peoples' feelings. Their feelings are up to them.

About two weeks after implementing boundaries I was in the shower bathing a resident in the hydraulic bath tub. I had the curtain pulled around us for privacy. My bath aid partner walked in and whipped the curtain back, saying, "What's goin' on Nancy?" I said, "Nothing. I am bathing Mr. so and so." She said it again and I said, "There is nothing going on." My boundaries were driving her crazy. While she was getting all spun up I was experiencing a sense of calm. *Hey, there's a freedom in this...*

When I started using my new-found boundaries with relatives, with my mother in particular, it sent a ripple through our entire family. One day I said no to an unreasonable request. As I replied I was polite and offered a suggestion on how to get her need met in some other way. *You want me to perm your hair? Uh, this could end badly. I'm not a beautician!* It wasn't the *need* not being met that was the problem – it was the *no* that started a chain reaction. My siblings were even calling me wondering what I'd done to mom. I even got a *shame on you* from my older brother. *Whatever.*

It took almost a year of re-establishing our relationship with the new terms in place. I am an individual and also an adult. Now and then I may say no and that's actually okay. I don't need to give a detailed explanation. Yes it was a bit awkward at first but I must give my mom credit. She respected my boundaries for the most part. This was new, necessary and healthy. It was a step in the right direction. Oh, but there was so much more to learn.

During this period of my life (and thanks to the antagonistic co-worker God used to propel me from my comfort zone to yet another world of the unknown) I'd bought a massage gift certificate for someone. Never having had one myself I felt it might be something they would enjoy. I was mistaken though and it never got used. The gift recipient equated touch to sex (as did I at the time) so him getting a professional massage was never going to happen. The certificate wasn't cheap. It cost me $45.00 and I got to thinking, *hmmm...$45.00 per hour? I could do that.* Mind you, I had never given a massage nor ever received one, plus I had no idea what was involved at all! I am from an extremely non-touching family, so much so that at one time the idea of shaking someone's hand made me nervous and God forbid hugging. To be hugged or to hug someone made me down right nauseous. This did not stop me though.

During a conversation with the charge nurse at the nursing home I mentioned my idea of enrolling in massage school. She said six words that changed the course of my life forever: "You'd be good at that, Nancy." That was it. Those words coming from her meant so much to me. One, I respected her. Two, I knew that was as much encouragement as I was going to get. Earlier when I had completed three quarters of college my field of interest was psychology. When I mentioned this to my mother all she said was, "Why do you want to be a quack?" As you know I eventually ended my college stint to be trained as a certified nurse's assistant and began working at the nursing home. Knowing my decision to go into the massage therapy field would be met with more criticism or sarcasm and little family support I didn't share my plans right away. Just like when I joined the Navy I was quite unaware of what I was getting myself into but dove in anyway.

My half-inch acrylic nails were looked upon with trepidation and distain by my fellow students. Their faces said *she's not getting anywhere near me with those!* Why I didn't equate massage with touching is beyond me. It just did not sink in that I would have to actually *massage* people! *Do I like touching people? Maybe if I don't have to shake their hand or hug them...*

I was thinking about the money, plain and simple. If I had really thought about what I was going to be doing—being touched by 20 strangers and touching them—I *never ever* would have signed the papers nor paid the money to attend massage school! But like most of my career choices I entered into it blindly without a lot of forethought. Had I inquired more carefully I may have chickened out. Maybe ignorance really is bliss. Ignorance had worked for me in the past and again it was proving to be most helpful.

During the first week of massage theory and practice we were asked to write on a 3x5 note card what we hoped to learn and get out of the class. I was becoming fascinated by the mind body connection and how they were directly and intricately interrelated with one another. Through the course work and practical application of it I soon began to experience intimately how we are so beautifully and wonderfully made. Today having been in practice as a licensed massage practitioner for going on twenty years this still never ceases to amaze me. During my schooling I would very often drive home in tears. The massages, even by novices that we were, were having a powerful effect on me, unlocking deeply-entrenched emotions I'd never experienced. I never got sad. I just got mad. Discovering there were more than two emotions (anger and happiness) was confusing at first. During one of our practical tests when I was being massaged the gal working on me began to slowly manipulate the muscles attached to my scapula. A flood of tears poured from my eyes and I was gripped with sadness. *Why am I crying? Where is this coming from?* My sobbing made *her* stop dead in her tracks. Another student said, "I can't handle this." By this time everyone in class was waiting to see if we were supposed to continue. They were, but we were not. It was suggested I get up and get dressed. I'd experienced an emotional release right there in the middle of a test. It came without warning and there was nothing I could do to stuff it back down.

Massage is a powerful tool for releasing buried hurts and emotions. Of course I couldn't identify what and where these were coming from that day. Shortly after I entered into counseling. It was helpful to a degree but not life altering. My eyes were beginning to be opened insofar as I was dating someone who was very much like my mother. She may not have been a drinker but she certainly had looking at the world through rose-colored glasses down to a fine art.

My radar for spotting (and being spotted by) addictive personalities was in full swing. I had starting seeing someone I'd met at the gym in 1995. He had a busy social life in Seattle on weekends so he stayed at my house Monday through Thursday. Four years into this thing I was listening to Laura Schlesinger on the radio and I realized I was a 'shack-up honey.' *Crap*. I also realized he was an alcoholic but I thought he'd change. He would realize he had a problem and he'd quit drinking, right? Notice a pattern here? There was no future with this person and my ten-year-old son's emotional maturity was surpassing this person's at a rapid rate.

Something was wrong. I broke it off for good but jumped into another fire. I quickly began an engagement with an ex-con who had a gambling problem. Not only that, but over the course of 4 to 5 weeks he displayed 13 of the 15 characteristics of an abuser listed in Dear Abby's column. Yes, I would have the honor of becoming the 5th Mrs. Felon (not his real name). If I hadn't foolishly let him move in after knowing him only two weeks I may not have been the recipient of his abusive traits (nor discovered them, yet). Although letting him move in was a terrible decision, I may not have come to my senses as fast if I had not.

Adding to the drama, relatives who received wedding invitations contacted my family members to inform them that this fellow was detained in their grocery store for stealing just recently. Lesson learned: yes, some people may confess their sins to you as though they have given up their life of crime and feel they are being *honest* with you. However the fact of the matter is they tell you *now* so when it comes to light *later* (and it always does) they can say they didn't lie, they just didn't tell you *everything*. I had sent dozens of invitations. When I realized who he truly was and that I was making a huge mistake I parked 10 blocks away from my house and wrote the 'due to irreconcilable differences the wedding has been permanently postponed' letters. I addressed them and mailed them out. You may wonder why I would gravitate toward someone like him. To be honest I did not know why at the time. Eventually I came to a place of brokenness about eight years into my walk with Jesus. The walls were coming down. *What is going on? Why do I keep doing this?* When you are ready you find that He has been ready and waiting to help you. I was ready. I needed to *go there*, wherever *there* was. Turns out *there* was called deliverance ministry.

Through Cleansing Stream, two Emotionally Free seminars and a full year in one-on-one counseling with a wise female Christian counselor, my counselor helped me see how I was making choices out of a sense of shame. Shame dictated the lifestyle I engaged in—drinking, drugs, sex, unhealthy relationships, etc.—from when I was a deflated, inferior-feeling teenage girl right on up to adulthood. A year earlier when I stumbled on the Christian music station, I had begun working on my relationship with the Lord in the privacy of my car but still I had no accountability. I also wasn't getting any biblical teaching. Thankfully I eventually discovered world-class pastors like David Jeremiah, Charles Stanley and John Mac Arthur, who spoke God's truth over me. *Christian music for over a year and now teaching by pastors. I'm working on getting to know God.* I was still far off from following the Lord but I was beginning to learn about Him. Often while singing along with songs I cried as they told of how much He loved me. The hard shell around my heart was cracking.

By this time I had moved from one town to another. Moving was my way of starting over but it didn't make a difference. I just started doing the same thing somewhere else. *Wherever I go, there I am.* My belief that I needed a man to complete me was ingrained in my brain. In fact at one point I thought a lobotomy would be the solution to all my problems. I knew I had this skewed, hard wired way of thinking. *I can't do things differently, choose more wisely, react with more self-control, but I must.*

Something had to happen. Something had to change. It was me, but it took a while and many more internet searches for Mr. Right. So many more in fact, that after a while it felt like I was shopping for a man. *Umm, let's see…5'10' or taller, funny, employed, likes animals. Oh, and must be a Christian.* If you do not know how many levels of 'Christianity' there are, do some internet dating. You'll soon see that it can range from *why yes, I love the LORD, in fact that's why the last girl I lived with didn't work out. She was an Atheist,* to descriptions like *Fuller Theological Seminary graduate, lead singer on worship team,* etc. This particular profile was so intriguing I answered it, but that comes a little later in the story.

Fortunately for me I had a 25 minute commute each way to work. One day as I was listening to David Jeremiah, at the end of his message he said, "Do not let this be a substitute for finding your own church family." *Uaagh!* I'd been completely content to 'go to church' in my car for the last three years. I was fine to stay out of a building with all of those hypocrites! *Now he had to go and say that!*

10

Don't Get in that Car!

"Hear, O my people, and I will warn you if you would but listen to me, O Israel." – Psalm 81:8

My friend and massage exchange partner was a Christian. Secretly I wondered why I hadn't been invited to her church. I knew my occupation wasn't fully understood or accepted by all, but I felt that if she was one and attended this particular church then at least I wouldn't be judged for that. So I did what any good, co-dependent would do and got on the internet to find a date that would meet me at church. I didn't want to go it alone, yet. As usual this date had an addiction. He called me shortly after we met at the church to say he felt like driving his truck into a ditch. "Why?" I asked, and he told me he'd gambled his entire paycheck away! I said, "Are you going to go to church next Sunday?" and he said no. I thought *that's funny, that is exactly where you should be.* I went though. The first day I walked into the sanctuary I knew I was where I belonged.

2008 was a great year, really it was. I know I have jumped ahead nine years but humor me please. In 2008 I attended a Woman's Touch Ministry get together. The speaker was a woman I'd never heard of before: Zoeann Wilke. She was a talented singer and speaker with the most unusual presentation. She was so real. I could feel (what I later came to understand as) the anointing, or presence of God. She talked about the Holy Spirit as though He were a person, imagine that. I'd been relating only to Jesus. I could easily imagine Him. In fact it's a little embarrassing, but while watching the Jesus video that had come out on VHS and was really popular at the time...I actually caught myself lusting (just a little bit) after Jesus' calves or at least the actor playing Him in the movie. So hearing her refer to the Holy Spirit over and over was foreign to me. She even said when she'd wake up in the morning she put her arms around Him (wrapping her arms around herself and squeezing) and say, "Good morning, Holy Spirit!"

At the end of her talk she had us form a line with two sides. Each of us could walk down between the women on each side and they could pray for us as they felt led. I felt prompted to touch each woman as she passed by me and pray something very specific. These were not women I knew and I certainly didn't know what each of them needed to hear. But someone did: the Holy Spirit. Now it was my turn to go through the line and as I passed Zoanne, the speaker, she said, "Take your anointing and go, sister." I felt exhilarated after this event. I'd been exposed to the power of the Holy Spirit. Exposed sounds so impersonal though. I met the person of the Holy Spirit that day though this woman and I am truly forever grateful to her and this group of women that brought her to our community to speak that day.

Even after this though I'd fall back into the pattern of *trying*. Trying isn't a bad thing, like when you try to exercise more often, or try to be a better listener, or try to live within a budget (by the way all of these things are more doable with the help of the Holy Spirit). But what I'd *try* to do is everything (working, parenting, ministries, relationships) without the help of the Holy Spirit. The breakthrough I needed hadn't fully come yet. There had been a lot of growing in the area of trusting the Word, knowing Jesus but still I hadn't succumbed to the idea there was more. However I'd started to see there was through the experiences that seemed to come one right after the other. Wednesday night services are special. I firmly believe that God blesses those who make it to a service other than the one on Sunday. He just does. He knows you are there for Him. You want more of Him. You can't get enough of Him. You don't feel obligated to be there – you want to!

This particular evening the Pastor had us look up and read Thessalonians 5. This was a bit unusual for him to incorporate the congregation into his teaching. More often he spoke to us from the Word and did not leave us on our own to read a chapter, but he was teaching us that night to listen to the Spirit of God for ourselves (fancy that), which is often how he referred to the Holy Spirit as. I got down to verses 19 through 21, and my spirit just went *ah-ha*! There was a distraction I'd been dealing with and these verses spoke right to it.

Just recently I had been pursued by a fellow at church. This was all new to me. He and his girlfriend, I might add, were fairly new comers. They were interesting people, constantly by each other's side, arriving and departing together. When he first approached me it was during my watch as a prayer guard. I was a prayer guard captain and oversaw the prayer guard during our 10:00 am services every other week. He popped the question, "Would you like to go out sometime?" It was odd that he would approach me at this time, during prayer. Even more I thought it peculiar that he would ask me out at all because it was common knowledge he was seeing this woman he was with every Sunday. I was in shock and knocked off guard for the moment.

When I regained my composure and the blood finally drained from my warm blushing cheeks, I asked him, "Uh, what about Deborah?" He said, "She is very dear to me and a wonderful companion." I was thinking *yeah that is what I thought. So why are you asking me out?* I'd like to say that is what I asked him out loud, but what I said instead was, "Uh, let me think about it." There were a couple reasons for this response. First, I had not been asked out in person by anyone in several years, let alone by a believer. Another reason was I felt flattered – probably because he was already seeing someone else and I had actually been 'picked' to be his next conquest. This tapped into my deep insecurities of always being compared and here I was being chosen over someone else. Yes, it is sad and kind of sick but that is where my thought process was still at.

I'm relieved to say it didn't take long for me to make the *right* decision about how to respond. I even sought wise counsel. Being a long-time single woman who was learning more about who she was in the Lord and how to navigate this new experience, I asked a female pastor how I should respond. She very insightfully asked if I was interested in the man. I said, "Not really," and explained that I was more flattered by being asked out than interested. This conversation helped put things in the proper perspective. And if that wasn't enough I had a dream-vision (I am not sure which) where I was walking along a road and a car came by. It pulled over and inside was this couple – the man who asked me out and his girlfriend. They were saying to me, "Get in Nancy. You don't have to walk. We'll give you a ride." I heard the Lord saying, *Do Not Get Into That Car Nancy. Do Not Get In.*

The next Sunday I approached this man and said my answer was no. I could not go out with him. He seemed very surprised. Not long after this he appeared in church with a different woman. His regular 'girlfriend' still attended and seemed to give him his space and allow for this period he needed to go through. Not long after though he was back together with Deborah, they announced their engagement and got married.

As far as the verse in Thessalonians 5:19-21 goes, it says, *"Do not put out the Spirit's fire; do not treat prophesies with contempt. Test everything. Hold onto the good. Avoid every kind of evil."* I had been consumed with this situation. I'd really been pressing in to the Lord prior to this and now my time was spent grappling with all kinds of whys and how comes. My whole focus was drawn away from my walk with Jesus (remember in my dream I was walking along the road). It didn't make sense. It was confusing. It occurred to me this whole thing was dousing the fire in my soul. I always got fed on Wednesday nights but this particular teaching was a special order from the Holy Spirit prepared in advance for me to partake of. *I hear You, Lord. No more distractions.* Just what I needed at just the right time.

I was beginning to hear Him speak to me in a variety of ways. His will and purpose were frequently having to break through barriers I'd erected over the course of my life. His constant pursuing of me was humbling. But that's what He does. That's how He rolls. Oh, how He loves us!

11

Accountability on Wheels

"Therefore, having put away falsehood, let each one of you speak the truth with his neighbor, for we are members one of another." – Ephesians 4:25

Let's jump back to 1999. God knows just what you need and when you need it. After churching myself for a couple of years in my car, yet still having no accountability and not a soul to really share all that was happening to me, who rolls into my life one day? Ann Williams. And I mean rolls. Ann was in a wheelchair and had been since she was 15 when she had an inner tubing accident at the Heart O' the Hills State Park in the Olympic National Forest. She was descending a snowy hill on a rented inner tube when her tube began to gain speed. Passing her friend, she continued her descent down two slopes eventually being stopped by a tree which broke her back and left her paralyzed in both legs. They calculated she was going approximately 60 miles an hour before slamming into the tree. Ann was now married with two beautiful kids. She said even though she was paralyzed she still experienced all the pain that went along with childbirth. She has an awe-inspiring life story she should write someday but in the meantime she is a larger than life Gospel spreader with the capacity to love like Jesus; to love like no one I've ever met. This is who God (by way of a gift certificate for massage) brought into my life when I needed a stalwart Christian role model that I could be discipled by, be accountable to and just plain enjoy.

Ann had been given a half hour gift certificate. I'd never massaged anyone in a wheelchair before so I worked on her and enjoyed the challenge. Later when she was rear-ended and was prescribed massage therapy she said she remembered me because I talked passionately (I think her words were non-stop) about my son and this impressed her. I ended up working on Ann in her home for many years. Meeting her there was easier since our parking lot was sloped.

The first time she came to see me in my office I saw her pull in and went outside to meet her. She parked. She reached over with her right hand and opened her passenger door. She then pushed forward the back of the passenger seat, then proceeded to grab her wheelchair in the back again with her right hand and fling her chair out of the car. She then scooted herself over to the passenger side, opened her wheelchair up (which had been in a folded position), locked the brakes and transferred herself into the chair. Realizing she would have to do all of this in reverse *after* her massage I offered to come to her home for all her subsequent treatments. And so that's how one of the best relationships of my life started. God knew I had trust issues with women. Our relationship started as a patient-practitioner one and grew into a friendship. With Ann there were no pretenses, no games, just Ann.

Accountability is HUGE. I can't say that enough. Up until I actually started attending church in 1999 and then getting into a women's small group in 2001, Ann was my *only* accountability other than the Holy Spirit. Until you've written God's Word on your heart so it's easy to retrieve on a regular basis, friends who *know* the Word of God are a necessary thing. The Holy Spirit gave me the wisdom to listen to Ann. Her influence on me was instrumental in my walk with Jesus from the very beginning. I don't see her very much anymore but she left an indelible mark on my life and I am so full of gratitude for her. I can't imagine how I would have fared without her in that season.

Thanks to another persistent woman at church (I'll call her Viv) I eventually joined a woman's group. Honestly I wasn't really keen on doing so but all my excuses were running out. She literally asked me to come at least once a month for a year and a half before I agreed. I was a baby Christian and when you are a babe you really don't see yourself that way. Like any stage of life you can't imagine how it will be when you are older or more mature. You just don't know what to expect. Same thing with growing in Christ.

When it came to joining a woman's group, I didn't really trust women. It was always easier talking to men. Growing up I never was in a clique or hung out with a particular group of girls but I knew what kind of malicious, slanderous talk can go on when a bunch of them get together. This church group was different – I know, I know. These were Christians, however I was still afraid. I was also concerned about sticking my foot in my mouth and not saying the 'right' thing. My manners, my responses or lack thereof were still causing problems.

I had opened a massage therapy practice in downtown Bremerton, Washington. When I went to scope out the practitioner room for rent there were four rooms available. The price was right so I snatched them all up. It didn't take long to find other LMP's who also wanted to rent a room. I sublet to a couple LMP's who had worked with each other at another location. As time went on there seemed to be a growing tension in the air. They were very tight friends and I could sense something was going on behind my back, so to speak.

During one of the first few times attending the women's fellowship group I began to share about this situation at my office. Usually we'd study the message the Pastor gave the previous Sunday and talk about how we've applied it or related to it. At the end we'd then share our praise reports and prayer requests. I told of my work situation and asked for prayer. Through the teaching we were studying and being open to the Lord and allowing Him to speak into my life I realized I had very poor communication skills. I could handle one-on-one just fine, however managing an office with multiple therapists was proving to be a challenge for me and made my deficiencies glaringly apparent. I realized I had not talked to these two ladies...hardly at all. I didn't want to get in between them so I simply avoided them. *Am I somehow scared of them?* They had been wanting a meeting with me. Finally I gave them the opportunity to speak to me.

All three of us sat down in the waiting area of the office. I started by saying, "I apologize for not communicating with you. It is not my strong suit. I want you to know I would be very hurt if you plan on leaving Affinity (the name of the business) and relocating to the other side of the building. If Terry (the landlord) allows you to then I will pack up and leave first." I had a sense this is what they wanted to talk to me about and sure enough it was. After I shared my feelings one of then spoke and admitted that is what they were thinking about doing but as of that moment she'd decided against it.

I have to tell you, God literally gave me those words to say. I would never have been able to share my feelings nor be so bold as to declare *I* would leave. But those are the words that came out of my mouth that day and since then one of them has been my right arm in the operating of the business. Because of my authentic communication she began to trust me that day. She was there more often than I. I had her take care of interactions with our landlord. She'd always ask me for my okay first. We had other LMP's come and go and she helped with those transitions, as well. A couple of years ago I turned the business over to her and now I rent from her! I couldn't be happier. I was able to go back to my ladies after that meeting and share how God showed up, gave me the words to say and the heart to say them with conviction as well as with concern. Everything God does deserves to be shared. It encourages others to know their prayers helped. It reinforces the reality that His constant hand is in our affairs – the ones we invite Him into and even ones we don't.

12

Earlier Church Attempt

"Let us not give up the habit of meeting together, as some are doing..." – Hebrews 10:25

My son was 12 when we started attending church. The game room that housed video games was a big help. I can't imagine all the things he thought and felt being that age never having gone to church before. Well, I suppose we had tried to twice before – the first time when he was just 23 months old. We'd moved in with my folks after I was discharged from the Navy. My dad flew to Maryland and helped with the final details of packing out and turning over the house my late husband and I had bought in 1988. Leo, dad and I drove across country to Washington State together. We stayed with them until I was hired by a contracting outfit in Kitsap County and moved to Silverdale. While at my parents' in Redmond, Washington we attended Overlake Christian Church. We stopped by the crowded nursery. Peering in through the glass, the sheer amount of babies in the room was overwhelming to me. Apparently for Leo, too. He stood there and looked at all the little ones and said, "Kids, kiiiids." His social phobias were already developing. We signed him in and off to the service we went.

The next time was early 1997. Leo was nine. I'd read *Mere Christianity* by C.S. Lewis. He is majorly responsible for my turn from New Age philosophy to Christian theology. Anyway, I decided I wanted to find a church, get baptized and get out. I had worked in downtown Silverdale and noticed a church next to one of the hair stylists I'd gone to – a very, very small church.

Leo and I were greeted as we entered by what later appeared to be the entire worship team – three people: two guitarists and a vocalist with a tambourine. We sat in one of the back pews, of course. When worship started they sang songs I hadn't heard of and the lady behind me was singing words that were not the same ones as the worship team's. In fact they weren't even in the same language. Leo later asked me why that lady was 'making sounds.' I didn't have an answer but I am sure I made up something. Next the pastor's wife started preaching/sharing. *WHOA wait a minute!* This was all new to me. *What is she doing?* This wasn't like the churches I went to growing up! Next her husband, a very, very attractive man about my age stood up and started preaching on lust or the evils thereof. *Hold on! I got a nine year old boy here. I don't think he needs to be hearing about this now!* He continued to read from Romans 7:21-25 and so on. Needless to say I did *not* get baptized that day. And it was another two and a half years (almost three) before I attempted church again.

13

My Son, Leo

"For you created my inmost being; you knit me together in my mother's womb." – Psalm 139:13

We moved from Silverdale to Bremerton in August 1997. Leo started third grade at a new school. One day he came home and told me he'd been beat up on the bus. Not only beat up that day but this was the second time it had happened. I was incensed! *Why isn't the bus driver doing something?* I was going to contact the principal and complain. But Leo said, "No, Mom. Wait until it happens again."

Leo had been diagnosed as ADHD at the end of his second grade year. His teacher, Mrs. Dori, bless her heart, adored Leo and appreciated his humor. She told me she could see him as a political cartoonist. He was eight. She had a 'Who Gets To Sit Next To Leo' weekly list. Apparently he was so fidgety and up and down so much the other kids had difficulty sitting next to him because of all the distractions. I knew he had problems focusing mainly because when he brought home math homework he could not complete a more than three digit addition problem without already being on the next one – not the next sequential one but one somewhere else on the homework page. His thought process was scattered. It was painful to watch and painful to try and help. My younger brother was ADHD. He was medicated but not for very long. I often thought if he had been on his meds longer he may have had a different life. This thought helped motivate me to do something for Leo but not right away.

It wasn't until he was beaten up twice on the bus that I realized I had to do something *now*. He started taking a very low dose of Dexedrine, a stimulant. The best description that helped me understand why a stimulant slows a hyperactive brain down is this: we have a 'governor' in our brain that receives signals from the outside. For an ADHD child this governor is slow and cannot handle all of the external stimuli, therefore causing impulsivity. The stimulant speeds up the governor making the brain capable of responding rather than reacting to the stimuli. 'Nuff said.

In two weeks' time my son's school life changed so dramatically that I knew I was doing the right thing by him. His teacher commented that he must have finally settled in because he was her star student. He'd finish his classwork first, as well. She would allow him to grade the papers of the other students. I let her know he was on new medication. It made all the difference in the world for him.

Later that year he was tested and accepted into the capable kids program. He would have to attend another school. I drove him everyday and this started our on-the-way-to-school conversations. Leo had difficulty making friends at his previous school, but once he arrived at his new school he made friends almost instantly. He was with like-minded boys. He is still friends with some of those boys today. This was such a blessing. Even though he had friends he'd never initiate getting together with any of them. I would have to threaten him and tell him if he didn't call one of them and invite him over, I would!

So began his foray into interpersonal relationships. It was great! He was still very often alone though, especially those hours immediately after school when he didn't have soccer practice. I'd opened my practice in Bremerton so that I could get him to and from soccer practice. I'd been trying to do this while practicing in Poulsbo alone. Driving like a bat out of hell trying to get home, pick him up, drop him off at the field, get back to Poulsbo 25 miles away, do a massage (because everyone wants a massage at 5:00 pm), get back to Bremerton before all the other moms picked up their sons and repeat this craziness two or three times a week.

Well, one dark rainy cold October night I arrived at the field to pick Leo up. I was probably 5 minutes late. His coach had him sitting in his van with the heater on. He came to my car window and said Leo was cold and didn't have a coat. Leo actually had plenty coats but he either wouldn't wear it or he'd take it off and lose it almost immediately. Leo got in the car and we drove home. I was determined to find an office in Bremerton that I could work out of on Tuesdays and Thursdays – soccer practice days. I looked at one place with a view of the Puget Sound in Bremerton. Beautiful location, however there was some ooze coming up out of the concrete floor. Creosote, I figured, and I couldn't with a clear conscience cover it with carpet and call it good knowing my clients would be breathing in that substance as I coached them *to take a deep breath. Nope, that won't do.*

Six months later I received a call from a man named Terry. He said he bought a building in Bremerton and was looking for tenants and asked if I would like to come see the rooms. The building was literally two miles from my house. It was old, funky and super inexpensive rent. I rented four rooms all on one wing. It was ideal. A couple of months later a Chiropractor called and said she had heard I owned this building and I may have a space she could rent. I told her I myself rented from Terry the landlord and gave her his number. She's been at the end of the hall ever since.

One day I felt I needed to go home. It was an overwhelming sense and dread was attached to it. I arrived home to find my son viewing the most hideous pornography online. We had internet and I was oblivious to what he'd been looking at. I noticed a change in him and chalked it up to puberty. My heart broke. His innocence was gone. Come to find out he had been introduced to porn when he was only nine at his bus stop. A boy brought magazines and Leo brought them home. He had a tree fort in the backyard. That's where he kept them. A person knows when they are doing something wrong. It is a natural instinct to hide just like Adam and Eve did in the garden. Our God-given conscience says *this is bad.* And it is. It is bad for us and it breaks God's heart when we choose darkness rather than light.

That day I got a glimpse of the heart break the Father feels when we choose things that harm us; things that don't help or heal us. My eyes were suddenly opened to how I was not there for my son. It was devastating to look back at my work schedule and see how I had put my clients' needs before my son's. *Oh how many hours I had left him home alone.* Worse yet, when I was home I had been more like a warden than a mom. Homework, homework, homework seemed to be all I focused on; on doing not being. God let me see something very hard to own. He let me see how I compared my son to other boys. Not necessarily saying anything to his face, but my inflections, tone and the judgmental attitude behind them said *why aren't you like other boys*! No, I didn't want to be this way! *I love my son! He is good enough!*

I saw how I was passing on the shame I felt for not being like so and so. *No God! I don't want to do that!* That day HE broke my heart. HE gave me a new heart for my boy. I told God if I change my schedule to accommodate Leo's He'd have to fill it, because who wants a massage at 9:00 am? Apparently a lot of people do, because it became one of my most popular appointment times. In fact my schedule started filling up and I was booked out further than I had been before. A message on one of the talk radio shows I listened to spoke on how to parent well, you have to be there. You know there is only one letter difference in present and parent? I had to be present as a parent.

My new schedule made it so I was home when he got home. On Wednesdays I started working half days so I could be there after school. I started working on my relationship with Leo and being less concerned with his homework. I had been learning about being present, giving attention to what you are doing at that moment; being in the moment with people. Now I was working on that with my son. I began to see how unique this wonderful boy was. Leo couldn't (nor shouldn't) be shoved into a box and expected to be like other kids. He was one of a kind as we all are. And he was mine to love and help become a man. Oh, that realization was scary.

Being 15, I let him fly alone to Florida to meet my cousin and her grandkids. They were going to Disneyworld! Plus their condo complex had three pools and tons of fun. After a week I received a call from Leo. He left a message that said, "Hi,

Mom. Don't pick me up – I am staying!" There was something in his voice I had *never* heard before: GLEE! I was thrilled for him and decided to let him stay longer. When I attempted to call back he was out swimming so I left a message: "When are you coming home?" A few days went by and no call. He was in good hands.

My cousin Kathy who was in her 60's at the time had umpteen grandkids and was the grandma of all grandmas. Her age was only a number (and one she would lie about if you asked her). She was a responsible, loving, big kid herself. I was so delighted he was enjoying himself and I couldn't get the sound of his joyful voice out of my head. Glee! I discovered that the gang had left Florida and were now back in Virginia. Leo was staying with my cousin's daughter. She had a son who was five years older than Leo and they just clicked. Still I had not been able to talk to Leo directly. The weekend of my niece's wedding was quickly approaching and we needed to fly to California. *I need that boy home!* Finally I called and said, "He needs to be on a plane by Thursday because we are flying to California Friday!" Sure enough they sent him back just in time. He'd even bought a journal and started chronicling his life at the ripe old age of 15.

After he returned Leo and I were having some difficulties. He was doing what kids do at that age: trying to establish their identity. I felt I had run the course as far as what I could do for a growing boy who was becoming a young man. Remembering how happy he sounded while in Florida, I thought Kathy and her husband Johnny are two very strong, loving Christians, *maybe they could take it from here? Besides, what did I have to offer?* I didn't know what a 15-year- old boy needed. So I e-mailed Kathy and asked her if she and Johnny would take Leo in and raise him the rest of the way through high school. *Oh, and don't worry about finances he comes with a social security check as his late father's dependent.* For days...nothing. I heard nothing back.

I had my mom and dad over for dinner and I told her of my plan, my e-mail and about how Leo was full of glee when he was in Florida with Kathy and family. Leo, from the other room where he usually sat in front of the computer eating dinner said, "I was on vacation, mom, and I was away from you. What's not to be gleeful about!" My mom mentioned an article she'd recently read (probably in *Reader's Digest*) of men whose mothers abandoned them in times of crisis. These men were successful now, but the one thing they *never* got over was being abandoned by their moms. So I said, "Okay, I'll keep him, but he was so full of gleeeeeeee!" Shortly afterwards I e-mailed my cousin Kathy and told her of my decision to keep him with me. I received an e-mail reply two seconds later saying, "We would have taken him." I think her inner wisdom said to give me time to really think about what I'd asked her. She knew I'd come to my senses.

14

His Mysterious Ways

"The Lord our God is merciful and forgiving even though we have rebelled against him." – Daniel 9:9

Leo still had some issues to work through. I heard of a book called *Every Young Man's Battle* and purchased it. I wanted Leo to read it but I read it first. It spoke of how males are visual and how they viewed women was by design. It was in God's plan that a man would be attracted to a woman and her differences. But everything relating to sexuality became distorted after the 'fall of man' in the Garden of Eden. This fascinating book opened my eyes to how I viewed myself and men, and even other women. It spoke to my heart on levels I couldn't imagine.

You see, after I got out of the Navy I had plenty of money and time and went out and did something I had wanted to do while still in the Navy. Before my husband died I'd had a consultation about getting breast implants. They performed cosmetic procedures at Bethesda Military Hospital. I was set to schedule my implant surgery when the first Iraq conflict was set to begin. Due to the timing they recalled all elective surgeries. After I was widowed I was still bent on getting those implants. So in December 1990, I did. Five years later I had to have them, well...let's just say 'adjusted.' One was trying to become a shoulder pad while the other was migrating under my arm pit. Not good.

After having come to know Jesus my eyes were being opened, albeit slowly. I think this is what it means when God says He doesn't give you more than you can handle. He doesn't reveal those things about yourself to you *until* you can receive them in the spirit with which He wants to impart them. Eeeyoooowah! Yes, it hit me! I compared myself to other women based on the reaction I would get from men. I saw how I was using an enhanced version of what God gave me purely for the purpose of luring men into noticing me. With this revelation I didn't feel shame though. I felt convicted. Conviction moves us in the right direction. Shame either paralyzes us to do nothing or causes us to go down a road of death and destruction. That's the difference between what God wants to do in your life and what Satan wants.

Even though I had come a long way I was still not completely on the right track with the guy thing. For some reason (I didn't have to guess now) the neighbor who was nine years my junior took notice of me. He was a painter and had some problems. In fact he was in jail when I first moved in and I didn't know who he was for a year or more. He owned his own paint company and had been a painter since he was 15. There was a certain charm about him that said *bad boy* all over it and I was interested in what made him tick.

He took me to a jazz/techno fusion club in Tacoma one evening. I took him out to meet the folks. My dad liked him right away. He was personable but I noticed something odd one morning when he came over for coffee. As he stood on my porch surveying the territory (as though he'd conquered new ground) there seemed to be a sense of entitlement...no, a sense of ownership as he smiled, gazing at my yard and his just beyond. The night before he had pulled me toward him jarring my chest up against his. He was strong and forceful and I didn't like this. After coffee I went about my day and hit the gym hard that night. I used a machine for my pectorals (chest muscles) which I hadn't used in a while. The next morning when I tried to roll out of bed the most excruciating pain stopped me cold. It was so painful. My left side felt as though I'd been hit by a truck. I think between his thrusting up against me and using the pec equipment something tore.

Somehow I must have had a micro sized cut in my hand or foot that allowed bacteria to enter my body. Eventually my left breast swelled to twice its size and now had a red ring around it. I'd been to the plastic surgeon just two months before wanting to have my implants removed. This doctor was hesitant. He wondered why I'd want to do something like that since I had a perfect outcome. "Well, no," I said. "I had to come back five years later and have them fixed." In a condescending tone, he said, "Well, you aren't having any problems now. Why don't you go home and think about it." *Uh, doesn't he know I've already done that?! I took a full day off of work to make the trip all the way over here!*

I certainly had thought about it. Maybe his pride wouldn't allow him to undo something he did that didn't have a problem. The surgery would have cost upwards of $4000.00 which I really didn't have but I was convicted and wanted them gone! My cousin who came with me was waiting outside, smoking. When I emerged from his office she asked, "What did he say?" "Go home and think about," I mumbled. "I thought you already did?" she asked with a raised eyebrow. "Yes, so did I."

Two months later there I was in his office again. When his nurse saw my breast her face registered aghast. When he looked his poker face just said...nothing. "What did you do?" he asked.

I told him about the pec machine, not the other. He put me on a 10-day regimen of strong antibiotics and said to return after the prescription was complete. I did and he put me on another 10 days of the same antibiotic. The infection was not completely resolved. To make a long story short, I spoke to a surgeon about removing my implants. X-rays were taken and when I saw those glowing white orbs in the images I knew those had to come out. He noticed that I used the VA (Veterans Administration) for health care and asked if I had checked with them about the removal of the implants. "They could do it a lot cheaper." I had not even considered that.

I followed up on his advice with a phone call then a consultation, and a couple of short months later I was having University of Washington surgeons (contracted with the VA) remove my implants. Beforehand they even offered to swap them out for saline ones instead. "No thanks," I said. Because I still had some residual infection in the left breast they deemed the surgery medically necessary. Between my private pay (that would not have covered 'elective' surgery) and the VA the price tag for the surgical removal was zero. *Zero!* God honors decisions you make that honor Him. Only He could allow what seemed like brazen disobedience—my decision against my better judgment to get mixed up with my neighbor—to turn out to benefit me in the long run by way of contracting a bacterial infection, that led me from one surgeon (who honestly didn't have to suggest I go somewhere else since surgery is how they generate their income) to a facility that used top-rated surgeons and getting a bill for zero...zip. Only God, a loving, personal God!

15

Your Mission is Leo

"A father to the fatherless, a defender of widows, is God in his Holy dwelling." – Psalm 68:5

I believed God when He said He would be the Father to the fatherless. Now more than ever I was praying for Leo. What exactly he needed, I wasn't sure. My prayers were that God would provide what a boy needs at this stage in life. My prayer wasn't specific. After all God knew my son and loved him even more than me. I wanted for him what God thought was best. He knows what we need more than we do.

Soon after agreeing to keep Leo at home there was a change in staff at church. Our youth department hired two new youth pastors. One had been a member of the congregation for quite some time. He was a little older, a little wiser. The other was this hip, 20-something, married young man. Leo took a liking to him right away. He looked forward to going to youth group each week. These two men took an interest in Leo. They genuinely liked him and Leo knew it. One would invite him to his apartment where he and his wife lived to watch a movie. He'd stop by and play Halo with Leo and pick him up to do random errands, like buy tires. The other didn't cut Leo any slack. He enjoyed Leo's quick wit and sense of humor.

Our house seemed to be the teenage hang out place. Kids always gravitate to where they feel accepted and joyfully that was our home. One time, Ben, the younger youth pastor stopped by for an impromptu visit. There were probably three boys plus Leo at the house all playing a World of Warcraft video game with each other on their individual laptops. He was amazed and pleased to see this going on and gave me kudos for being there. I was always there. If Leo was home generally I was, too. I loved being there, being available. I was Mom, not friend. There were rules and lines and 99% of the time they were not crossed. Our relationship was in a good place and I was so enjoying him now. This is not to say he didn't ever try to push my buttons. He did...every chance he got. Being brilliant at doing so used to drive me crazy but now it was more of an annoyance than anything else. His opinion of me didn't influence my responses and rules like it once did. I was the adult, the parent and the 'heavy' now and then. Daily I sought the Lord for when to push in when to pull back. It is a fine line with a child that age and I think he knew it, too.

One time however, after he'd gotten his license and was broadening the gap that separates mother and son (that oh-so-necessary degree of separation, allowing a boy to inch toward manhood), in my need to control his environment I almost made a fatal mistake. He wanted to go somewhere in his new car and he was so excited about it. I heard myself delivering a guilt-ridden schpeal (spun from fear) and literally pouring rotten, stinking, sour vibes all over what should have been one of his best first memories with his new-found freedom. My mind ran wild with worst-case scenarios. I imagined him drinking and driving, getting smashed and ending up somewhere with someone he didn't even know...*Wait! This is Leo, not me – teenage Nancy who had a death wish. My freedom caused more crazy, but Leo isn't me.* Memories of each time I got into my car had surfaced, like getting drunk and ending up somewhere with someone I didn't know. *NO, this is Leo.* I had to literally have a conversation with myself. *Nancy, what are you doing? Why are you spoiling his fun? Let him go. Trust him. He's not you!*

Leo was a gem. He would have complied with my fears and stayed home. *Nooooooo*...instead I changed my tune and salvaged the memory that was going to take place. After he took the keys and left I recognized how often I had sabotaged my own moments of fun with negative expectations; expecting the worst. Even if it made me miserable it was a way to control or so I thought. God opened my eyes. There and then with Leo was a defining moment in my ability to let him go a little more, encouraging his maturity and freedom. I never wanted him to want to stay home with me or to feel obligated to. He needed to spread his wings and jump. He might not fly right away but I wanted him to want to give it a try. *Fly, son! Practice getting out of the nest and eventually stay out for your sake and mine.* Isn't that what we should want for our sons and daughters? Isn't that what God wants for his kids?

He trains us up in the way we should go, giving us the Bible, leading us to participate in fellowship and having conversations with Him in prayer. He says, "Trust Me, I know what is best for you. I want you to not only have life, but an abundant life!" Steps of faith are us telling God we trust Him; even small steps. What does God do when we trust Him? He keeps His promises. The only way to know what His promises are is to know His Word which He has provided. What does His Word provide us with? The understanding of who He is. How do we begin to understand who He is? By knowing His Word and stepping out in faith by trusting Him. How do you know God? Well, how do you know anyone? By spending time together; by spending time with Him. How do you spend time with Him? By reading His Word, praying (talking) to Him and getting together with those who know Him. I also use a daily devotions book that has writings from those who have known God in the most intimate way. These former theologians—pastors, Christians of old whose lives reflected that of those who knew and served God well—were and are my mentors. Their insights and poems would lift me up when I was down. Before I began reading the Bible on a consistent basis my daily devotional book (with its daily scripture at the top and wise counsel from those that had lived in times past) encouraged me and gave me hope. Some of the writings would speak to my circumstance at exactly the right time. Of course the verses did as well but knowing that a regular human (not an apostle or disciple) wrote it made it seem more relevant to me at times.

During a small group an interesting question was posed: What do you think your mission is? What I heard the Lord say to me that day was, *Leo is your mission.* Leo had four more years of high school. That statement helped me understand I was to focus on my son, making sure he got what he needed from me without any competition.

16

Band of Gypsies

"So then, just as you received Jesus Christ as Lord, continue to live in him, rooted and built up in him, strengthened in the faith as you were taught, and overflowing with thankfulness." – Colossians 2:8

I had been celibate since 1999. Celibacy was a choice and a gift. I had asked God for it back when I was seduced by an ex-boyfriend once even after I received Jesus as my Lord and Savior. This was back when I had no accountability in my life. I made the mistake of allowing someone I'd had an on and off relationship with for four years to weasel his way back into my life and unfortunately into my bed.

He, the enemy, does prowl around like a lion just waiting to devour believers. It is his job to confuse us, confound us and ultimately destroy us. I experienced the chasm of separation from Jesus after my mistake. It was immediate – like the cord that connected me to Him had been severed. My sin and shame had severed the communion with Jesus with one fell swoop of fornication. It was ugly. It devastated me. That sweet presence I had been enjoying vanished in an instant. It was so powerful and so profound, I vowed *never again*! I felt I couldn't trust myself so I asked God for the gift of celibacy and He blessed me with it. The temptation never emerged until years and years later. Giving Him my attention (diverted from seeking a mate) had huge benefits. I focused on my relationship with the Lord. Relationships with women also started to flourish.

A dear friend included me in her outings. Eventually we formed a foursome and called ourselves the B.A.G.'s, short for Band of Gypsies. We'd go to plays in Tacoma or Seattle and often have dinner before the show or go shopping afterward at stores not found in our area. Other ladies heard about these trips. Our reputation for knowing how to have fun spread at church. If one of us could not go we'd allow an honorary BAG to take that place. I was the driver most of the time. My SUV was comfortable and we were good to go no matter the weather. My friend also hosted her yearly *No Valentine and Doing Fine* party around Valentine's Day. These parties consisted of lots of chocolate and in a creative way we'd encourage each other.

One time fruit was used as the object with which to express what you thought about another woman at the party. I was described as a pomegranate by one woman. She said I had as many facets to my personality as a pomegranate has seeds and that I was beautiful and unusual. I liked this. Knowing she knew me pretty well, as she was one of the BAG's, gave the words more value than had she been just an acquaintance. These women filled a void in my life. As a believer I was still growing and their friendship did more for me than any relationship with a man could. I was learning about myself through them. It seemed that God was using my independence, helping me realize that I didn't have to have a man to cultivate real relationships with women and other men.

I also began to understand the fine lines of familiarity and how you don't cross them with other women's husbands. It is inappropriate to enter that space of a man who is married. Even if it isn't flirtatious or sexual in any way, being too familiar is wrong. I paid attention and used cues to inform myself if I was invading someone's territory. Every now and then I still catch myself and draw back right away. In high school having guys as friends felt more comfortable than girls. Females can be fickle, catty and just plain mean at times. Hanging out with guys was easier. But the lines and boundaries are to be respected. I stay on guard and practice vigilance when it comes to interaction with men in the church or outside.

17

Unexpected Gifts

"He who did not spare his own Son, but gave him up for us all, how will he also along with him, graciously give us all things?" – Romans 8:32

Ecclesiastes 7:20 says, *"There is not a righteous man on earth who does what is right and never sins,"* and Romans 3:10 says, *"As it is written: There is no one righteous. Not even one."* These verses give me great consolation. My struggle with feeling accepted and worthy (and even just okay) can be constant. God is faithful to finish the work He has started. He says I am accepted despite the journey that remains ahead and I can look behind me and see where I have come from. That alone excites me, knowing He's going to be working in, on and through me until I see Him face to face. He is so gracious though. He won't barge in and say, "Look, Nancy, you really need to let go of this thing or that thing." No, He sheds His light, His unconditional loving light, on an idea, perception, prejudice, critical way or bad habit and says, *Hey, maybe you ought to know this,* or *I think you are ready to know that about yourself.* He uses people often to point out faults you might not be aware of, too. We all have our blind spots.

In 2007 I had a client who, in her first visit said to me, "We are going to be good friends." She is a counselor and knows about the patient-client relationship. One is there for therapy, the other is there to receive it. I made it a point to have my boundaries in place, knowing by this comment that they would be challenged and they were. We were from different belief systems and mind sets. I discovered that I would divulge more about me than I wanted. The massages became physically and mentally draining.

Her appointments were the same time and day of the week. She began calling the day of her massage to ask when it was just before her appointment time. I would tell her and she would then say she could not make it. The third time she called and said, "I know I do not have an appointment today but if I did, I wouldn't be able to keep it." I was agitated and my tone reflected it. I said to her she did, in fact, have an appointment today at 1:00. Of course she was unable to make it. I left my office and headed to my friend Ann's house to give her a massage. My phone rang again and it was my client who had just cancelled. She started by saying she felt as though she had to walk on egg shells around me. This may have been because she was a counselor to AIDS patients. She and I disagreed on some of her case management with one of her clients. My disagreement was voiced by not saying anything and a counselor knows silence speaks volumes. She was even adversarial at times about my faith and challenged things that placed me in a position to defend. Giving a massage is *not* the time to talk religion, politics or any other emotionally-charged topic especially if you are on opposite ends of the spectrum.

On the phone she continued, "I am cancelling all of my appointments and I am going to give you a gift: YOU DON'T KNOW HOW TO TALK TO PEOPLE." I was hurt, but managed to compose myself and said I would consider her words and thanked her for sharing and hung up. Her comments offended me. I had excuses for my tone. I knew I was justified when I spoke to her with an attitude. I was glad I was seeing Ann soon. *I will share what went on and she will defend me.* She did.

Later that week I was giving a massage to my dear friend and massage exchange partner, Suza. I relayed the story of the "gift." When I was working on her feet she said, "Well, there have been times when you've said something to me that hurt." *WHAT!?* Tears began to roll down my cheeks. Here was my good friend, someone I saw every two weeks for years for massage exchanges and who I hung out with…telling me I've hurt her with my words. I continued to massage. She could hear my sobs and said, "Wait, stop. I can't get massaged if you are crying." She went on to say it wasn't often, but it has happened and she thought I'd want to know. This coming from someone I knew and loved made me examine myself in a very different way.

I started paying attention to how I was feeling before I spoke to others, knowing my feelings would influence my tone and words. On the phone and even in person with clients I noticed I could be less than professional at times. My new goal became to treat my clients equally and with courtesy. Being tired greatly affected my ability to be cheerful so if I was tired I would postpone calling clients to schedule. With my friend I paid more attention and saw I could be short when I am familiar with someone, but that's not acceptable. *I never want to hurt these important people in my life.* Did that client really intend on giving me a gift? I don't really know her true motivation but she did nonetheless. Genesis 50:20 says, *"You intended to harm me, but God intends it for good to accomplish what is now being done, and saving many lives."*

18

Stretching, Feeling and Healing

"He heals the brokenhearted and binds up their wounds."
—Psalm 147:3

My son graduated from high school in 2007. He applied at the college of his choosing but found that his GPA was coming back to bite him. He began to apply himself in his senior year. Years of not being focused brought his grade point average down enough to limit his options. It was such a relief to have him graduate from high school. He eventually settled on starting his higher education at the local community college. Living at home he was able to work part time as well.

His next move was entirely up to him. If he wanted a degree he would have to go get it. No prodding from me. After his first year at Olympic College he decided to apply again to other four year colleges. He was accepted at Washington State University. We went for the orientation during the summer. The most ambitious and outgoing students volunteer to help for orientation week and Leo was impressed by one of the young men volunteers. Leo decided to enroll thinking he had a friend already. This fellow was a senior and in a fraternity. Later if he saw this charismatic senior on campus he sometimes said hello to Leo... sometimes.

Leo' class selection was extremely difficult. He failed two classes and did so poorly in others he couldn't register for the second semester without a conference first. I learned about this while he was home between semesters. I knew he wasn't doing well. When I picked him up during Thanksgiving break he climbed in the car saying, "Get me outta this God-forsaken place!" His appearance was startling. He was gaunt and pimply, not the healthy-looking 20 year old I'd dropped off just two and half months before. When he went back after Thanksgiving I let him take his car, which was a mistake. He refused to get a parking pass and had to move his car every 12 hours to avoid getting tickets! This contributed further to his depression. He coped by walking; walking for miles, gathering golf balls on his walks. By semester's end he had more than 500 balls he stored in a mesh bag. To celebrate the end of his first semester he set the golf balls free by rolling them down the dorm stairwell at 2:00 in the morning. Another indication he wouldn't be returning.

My cousin visited from Austria shortly after his homecoming. She took him out to lunch. When we were alone she said she knew why Leo did so poorly at WSU. I asked why. She said, "Because he missed his mommy."

Having raised six children I took her word for it. It wasn't his time to leave the nest. Yet, I had to give him credit. He did step out and try to fly. I was proud of him for that.

Now that he was growing up and moving on my focus turned inward. I'd been attending my church for seven years and had been serving in various ministries including the children's ministry, the prayer ministry and the women's ministry. A class I attended called *True Faced* really forced me to be more open and vulnerable with other women. I also began participating in the *Emotionally Free* seminars. Through the seminars I discovered the reason we can be saved and joined with God in Spirit yet struggle in our soul (mind and emotions). Apparently my promiscuity led to fragmentation of my soul by engaging in sexual activity with many different men over a period of time. God designed sex for one man and one women, husband and wife. It is sacred and not to be taken lightly. A bond is formed when you come together with another person. Sleeping with different people creates soul ties that, unless they are broken, are carried with you always as well as the shame that accompanies it.

Consciously I may not have acknowledged my actions as immoral but God writes His law on every heart. Just because I didn't admit to myself my choices were wrong doesn't mean I didn't realize they were at some level. Confessing of sins leads to repentance. I had confessed and asked for forgiveness during a Cleansing Stream retreat, recording each man's name (those I could remember), but the ties remained and needed to be broken. Did I think this was over-kill? Absolutely not. I also dealt with guilt I still carried regarding my husband's death. *Was my harsh mother-in-law right? Did I really break his heart and kill him?* I needed peace. I needed to know that my late husband didn't blame me. We can't communicate with the dead but Jesus can. Jesus gave me a peace that surpasses all understanding and I was relieved of that burden, too.

After participating in these seminars I became an assistant facilitator. This is when the Lord really began working on me in the area of letting go of control. I was to assist the prayer intercessor/facilitator who'd led my group in the past, Dr. Leigh Carol, PhD, psychologist. It wasn't her clinical skills or degree that frightened me but the way she went with the flow of the Holy Spirit. It defied all the training in the manual we followed. My comfort zone was obliterated and all I could do was hang on and trust I was hearing the Holy Spirit.

The very first time I co-facilitated we had a woman in the group who wanted to take over. Rather than simply participate her comfort zone was to help others get to the problem by asking them questions. I was feeling a bit displaced and began to question myself. *Perhaps I am not qualified and she'd do a better job.* My doubter kicked into high gear. Dr. Carol very gently reigned in the *helper*. I didn't share my thoughts with Dr. Carol that evening but she would have assured me I was the one meant to be assisting. Instead I went home and asked the Lord, a*m I qualified to do this? Maybe this other woman should take my place, Lord? Do I hear You, Lord?* I opened my Bible to John 10:3-4; *"He calls His own sheep by name and leads them out. When He has brought out all his own, He goes on ahead of them, and His sheep follow because they know His voice."* This spoke to my fear and it was dispelled. I *am* able to hear the Holy Spirit. I've been working on hearing Him more. Trusting was not something that came easily for me.

By this time I realized that although the emotional baggage I had carried with me for so long was finally getting addressed and I could help those that wanted to be emotionally free of theirs, there were still core issues I needed help getting to. This help came from a Christian counselor. She had her practice in the same building that housed our church. She didn't attend our church so there was some anonymity. I began counseling in 2008.

When I shared my lifestyle before becoming a Christian she ascertained I'd been looking for God and His love in a lot of different things: sex, drugs, alcohol, etc. I hadn't looked at it like that before, but when I considered it she was right. I used all those things to numb my overwhelming sense of inadequacy. They loosened me up to where I could be uninhibited enough to engage in the activity that spoke to me: physical contact. Without the substances my walls stayed firmly erected and no one could get past. I used to say jokingly that if it wasn't for drugs and alcohol I would still be a virgin. It isn't funny though. There *was* something I did at age 16 I have only shared with one other person on the planet. It is so repulsive to me and I will take it to the grave. Thank you, God, that I have been forgiven and that I no longer carry the shame that (at the time) led me further down the road of drinking and promiscuity.

I explored areas of my childhood with my counselor that gave me understanding to why I never felt good enough and why I put myself in situations with men that could have turned out *very* badly for me. I know I was protected, and even though I wasn't following Jesus at the time He was with me.

During the counseling I recalled an incident that took place when I was about five in our home in Tracyton. We called it the chocolate, strawberry and vanilla house because it was brown, pink and white. My parents were entertaining friends who had four daughters. I recall my older brother and one of the girls in a bedroom with me. There was touching involved and I was just this little girl that these older kids, 12 or 13 years old, were messing with. It is the only incident I remember. My innocence was gone from that point on. Sometimes it's not the incident that is as damaging as the reaction (or lack of) that sends the message you are not worthy, you are not good enough, you are not good. Shame is one of Satan's most effective weapons.

Shame is not simply a feeling although you can feel ashamed because of something you did or didn't do. No, I'd say it is like a systemic disease that attacks your very core. It's unforgiveness of self. It can either lie dormant or rage out of control, like what Admiral Boorda suffered when it was discovered he had falsely claimed he received certain honors which he hadn't. So deep was his shame, he killed himself. He couldn't live with it and he couldn't forgive himself. Had he not prided himself as an honorable man his dishonor may not have had the destructive, devastating effect on him that it did.

I never was able to acknowledge that I was full of shame. I didn't recognize that's what it was. The condition of my soul steered me in the direction of a lifestyle that could only be described as shameful. Shame led me there and then heaped more and more onto itself. First through therapeutic touch and later through Christ-centered prayer intervention and counseling with a Christian therapist, things I had stuffed, ignored and denied were at last unearthed.

When I began to receive massage therapy it was from fellow students. It wasn't necessarily a certain technique or style but the fact that I was being touched other than sexually which had an amazing effect on me. Also our muscles have memory. You may have heard that an athlete trains and works their muscles in order to establish the skill required to perform whatever sport they are competing in. Some countries, like Russia and China, begin training their athletes while they are still very young children. Not only does muscle memory record everything we do physically it also stores emotions. Getting massaged softened my tight musculature and it softened the hard exterior of my inner world. I had been so cut off from my emotions that when they finally surfaced, all I could do was cry, cry, cry. That's what I usually did on my way home from class.

God works in such wonderfully mysterious ways. He used my desire to make more money (by doing something I never could imagine myself doing in a million years) and turned it into the catalyst for breaking down walls erected long, long ago. Once the process of beginning to *feel* was set in motion, the process of beginning to *heal* was possible. When I stumbled on Christian radio my heart was in a vulnerable state. When a song spoke of Jesus and His love I could connect. As I sang along in my car tears would roll down my face. *Yes, I believe it. He really does love me.* Massage touch opened my feelings and the music's message could truly be received and believed: He loved me. He was knocking on my door and I was letting him in. I still had negative mindsets, seriously skewed and damaging beliefs about myself and not-so-healthy patterns that weren't healed overnight. But I discovered Someone who loved me enough to *die* for me; died so I could be transformed by washing away all of my sin (mistakes), and died so I could have relationship with the One who created me and who longed to have relationship with me. Jesus forgave me after everything I had done to myself and others. He forgave me.

Touch is a language. It is considered one of the five love languages. My family was not a touching family. There were no hugs or kisses. Touch was downright uncomfortable. So when I was *paid attention to* as a little girl by my older brother, this imprinted me, it spoke to me. It may have been wrong but it felt good to be noticed. That is a hook, a snare that was put in place. Unmet need meets sinful situation. The enemy always gets in and twists, distorts and just plain messes with what God created for good. Guilt and shame are attached to the hook – as if I had something to do with the events, as if they were partly my fault (which those early events were not). I've always had a sense that my family has an underlying secret; something untold, hidden, murky and messy. Something *not* good.

As I got older I became very self-conscious. When I was 11

my oldest sister got married. My other sister and I were her bridesmaids. I insisted on dress necklines that didn't plunge. In fact the dresses had neck lines that would be considered mock turtlenecks. They were custom made and that specification was a necessity in order for me to be comfortable enough to walk down an aisle in front of a hundred people. It wasn't until later that I wanted a figure that *would* get noticed. I was what you call a late-bloomer. When all of my friends were developing boobs and hips I wasn't yet. Being tall and thin was not desirable in my book. Names like Twiggy, String-bean, Olive Oyl and Stick Woman were testaments to my unwomanliness. I was so thin I wore thermal underwear under my jeans in order to bulk myself up. This was in warm Southern California, mind you.

Prior to leaving for the Navy I had a boyfriend. Remember the one who couldn't pay for dinner? That's the one. My dad had built a room in the garage for my older brother when he needed a place to stay. My brother had moved on and one night I had my boyfriend stay over. I asked my parents' permission and as long as he stayed in the garage room he could. I snuck out there (of course), not for the whole night but for a few minutes. A few nights later I was telling the folks I was going out. My dad said something to me that pierced my soul, "So you're going out to play grab butt?" His voice was filled with disgust. He had never spoken to me like this before. It felt accusatory and dirty. It was just a few weeks before my enlistment began. I actually liked this guy I was with and now it was something dirty. For a split second I thought I was worthy, normal. Someone liked me and I liked him back. Now it was dirty and shame-filled. I wrote him a couple times from boot-camp and he wrote me back. However by the time I was in A-school and surrounded and out-numbered by males, my old ways resumed and that was the end of our romance.

19

Rollercoaster Year

"Be joyful always, pray continually, give thanks in all circumstances; for this is God's will for you in Christ Jesus."
– 1 Thessalonians 5:16-18

The year 2008 was all about highs and lows. I'd begun counseling and the benefits were a high point. I'd had the encounter with Zoeann Wilke, the woman who said, "Take your anointing and go sister." What a high. I'd been pursued by a man at church who was dating another woman there... a weird low. Also I'd been working 12 years as a massage therapist: a career I loved and never tired of (definitely a high). My son was attending his first year at the community college. Another high. I had been exercising since 1991 (regularly for the most part). I was making it to the gym at least twice a week. I'd go in the evening after working all day. At some point during 2008 I decided that since I was going only two times a week, why go at all? So I quit. I also left my somewhat healthy way of eating and opted for eating whatever I wanted, whenever I wanted. I put on 13 pounds in six months. That was a low, sort of. It did give me a more shapely figure I'd always wanted but it also sent my blood sugars soaring.

My mom is type 2 diabetic as were both my grandmothers, at

least one uncle and a cousin. I had a physical at the VA where I received my health care and for months they were trying to contact me to come in for blood tests. They said my glucose levels were elevated. It took me awhile to make an appointment and get over to the VA hospital in Seattle. It required I take hours off from work to go and being self-employed and always needing to make money, I made excuses for not going. Well, after the tests they determined I now had type 2 diabetes. They prescribed orals and insulin. I brought home a meter with instructions how and when to test my blood. Type 2 they say *is* reversible. I set out to do just that.

I had a piece of exercise equipment and bought two more, used of course. I pretty much cut back on the obvious junk: candy, ice cream, cookies. So much so that when I awoke at 3:00 in the morning having low blood sugar I'd make my way to the kitchen for a big bowl of cereal. I never got the hang of using the insulin. It arced, meaning it was in my blood stream over a period of time and had a high point, then the level of it tapered off. If it sounds like I don't know what I am talking about, that's probably right. *How do I use this stuff and how does it work? Whatever...* A low glucose level, sometimes dangerously, was becoming routine. I ate so little sweet stuff that I almost looked forward to the big bowl of cereal I ate in the middle of the night to bring my blood sugar back up.

Towards the end of November my test strips ran out. To buy them over the counter is very expensive: $50 for fifty strips. I decided I would just watch what I ate and wing it. That turned out to be a big mistake. Over the course of 30 days I lost 23 pounds, my vision was often blurry and I was frequently wetting my bed. I found myself half lying down at the end of my massage table while I was working on a client's legs and feet. I remember thinking to myself, *it wasn't always this way*. Feeling awful was gradual. Thinking it was due to the diabetes didn't even occur to me. My energy level was minimal but I didn't miss a day of work, and I was still active in church. When I look back I know the Lord literally carried me during that time. My house and yard were neglected and I remember saying to my son that I needed his help with the lawn because I was sick.

Finally on my way to work one morning I called the VA and told them what I was experiencing. They said to come in right away and I did. I could tell by the look on my nurse's face that she was shocked by my appearance. My weight loss was not just the loss of fat but also muscle mass. When the body isn't getting the calories it needs to fuel itself it starts using up muscle. I was not just thin, but gaunt. After sending my blood to the University of Washington for testing I was told to stop the insulin and oral medications. Instead they issued me two new insulins to start taking immediately. My diagnosis was changed: type 1 diabetes or juvenile diabetes.

It's rare to get it later in life but it does happen. My energy level began to improve immediately. Very slowly my body began to gain weight which was a sign my body was getting the sugar it needed to function. Everything in our bodies runs off sugar and everything converts to sugar. How fast depends on the type of food. For a diabetic life is a series of highs and lows. The amount of fluctuation depends on how much control you have over your blood sugar. In the same way I believe our highs and lows in life depend on how much control we give to God. "In this world we will have trouble (lows), but He has overcome the world."

20

He Hasn't Called

"For my thoughts are not your thoughts, neither are your ways my ways." – Isaiah 55:8

Another high took place in 2008. I was a prayer team captain and one day our prayer group gathered to pray around the building next to our church. Leadership wanted God's direction whether to purchase it or not. It was a glass building so I thought to myself *it's a no brainier, it's cool, it's glass*. But we were asked to pray and pick up trash around it as we prayed. After praying we assembled upstairs where the pastor in charge prayed for us all prior to being dismissed. We all walked out, passing the church library and waved and said hello to the two gentlemen sitting in the room. Then I heard something surprising: *there's your husband, Nancy*. I recognized this voice, it was the same one that told me *Go home* when my son was in danger on the internet. It was His voice, the voice of the One who loves me unconditionally. I said to myself, *well, he's married* about the man on the left and *I don't know him* looking at the man on the right (who turned out to be David Duncan). We all left and at some point I told a friend about what I heard. She didn't say much and it was left at that.

A month had passed and no call from this supposed future husband of mine. Now my thought process started moving along those same old lines again...*I need a man*. Man-focused thinking wasn't always at the forefront anymore and I hadn't entertained the idea in years; four years to be exact. Leo was in college now. He definitely didn't need his mommy – he knew everything. You know how that goes. *Why not just look? Maybe God has someone for me now.* So I did.

On a Christian dating site (of course) I found Mr. Perfect. He had a Fuller Theological Seminary degree, he was a worship leader and attended a Four-Square church nearby. *Wow, jackpot.* We met. He was very nice and polite – a gentleman. He had interests like painting and music, with very specific tastes. Oh, and he cooked! He'd even worked as a cook previously.

As I got to know him I discovered some things that bothered me. I didn't want to be judgmental about his hobbies but some of them made me uneasy. During our first meeting he mentioned a drawing class he was taking...with nude models. *What?* At the time I thought this was okay. I reasoned, *he is an artist...artists draw different subjects.* His happen to be nudes. Later when he talked about a 19–year-old former gymnast—who wasn't a professional nude model—recently posing for his drawing class a red flag went up. I remember walking into church the Sunday after this revelation. While passing an associate pastor, an elder and then another associate pastor on the way in, in my mind I imagined asking them if they'd be okay with drawing a 19-year-old nude gymnast and each of their answers were a resounding *NO!*

It wasn't just his drawing nudes that stood out as something that was contrary to someone claiming to be following Christ and trying to live for Him. There was also the matter of his musical taste. Nightwish and Apocalyptica were two favorite bands of his. He took me to their concerts. I discovered the draw of metal music: it is pure adrenaline. By the end of the Apocolyptica concert I was flicking my Bic and yelling, "One more song!" I was hooked, and afterward on the way home I was looking up their concert dates and venues to see if we could make it to the next one. This music was tantalizing. There was a spiritual component, a hypnotic draw, and if I wasn't in my right mind I could have very easily become fanatical about their music. I truly could have. But I had chosen a different way to participate in life and it didn't include going to concerts where the music stirs you into a frenzy, leaving you wanting more of the music. No, I've chosen the person of Jesus Christ, God in flesh, who stirs up longings for more of Him, His peace, His hope and His joy.

We were listening to a CD by a German group on the way home. Since he spoke German I asked my date about what the lyrics were. He said, "Oh, he's singing about his girlfriend who is telling him she just wants to be friends." I don't know if that is really what the song was about or if my date was sensing a shift in me after the concert. I decided this relationship needed to end and the concert confirmed it. We'd spent about four months getting to know each other. We kept it platonic for a couple of reasons. One, I wasn't physically attracted to him. He had a kind face and he was soft spoken but there wasn't any chemistry, thankfully. Two, when I began to learn more about him I discovered that he was not who he presented himself to be. When I shared some of my experiences with a friend they said he sounded like a Counterfeit Christian. That was the first time I'd heard that term used. It was time to end it so I asked him to meet me at a popular pizza place. I told him that I couldn't see him anymore. He again was a gentleman and paid for the meal.

21

Rags to Righteousness

"Therefore, if anyone is in Christ Jesus he is a new creation; the old has gone, the new has come!" – 2 Corinthians 5:17

Sometime during our dating I had volunteered for a Saturday night prayer meeting at church. It was from 6:00-7:00 every Saturday evening. The Saturday after the breakup I was cleaning my basement. Start time was approaching and I felt a wave of dread come over me about going to the church to pray. My prayers seemed stilted compared to the others who showed up. They seemed to know something I didn't. *The others pray so much better than I do. Why bother going at all?* Feelings of inferiority and uselessness tugged at me. Staying home to finish cleaning the basement would have been much easier but I made a commitment and I keep my commitments. In an almost whiney, complaining voice I shouted out loud to God, "I have nothing to offer there. I don't know how to pray so You're going have to do it!" I was tired. Tired of trying. Tired of making the same old mistakes. Tired of being tired. So I went anyway with nothing to offer.

When I got there six or seven people had gathered plus the keyboardist. I've since discovered that nothing ushers in the presence of Jesus like worship music. We were all sitting in the front row off to the left by the keyboard. As we bowed our heads and the music began so did this vision.

I saw an ugly, filthy, holey sweater. Immediately I recognized the tattered sweater as being my old self. It was what I put on every day – trying in my strength, my own effort to be good *for* God but not trusting Him completely. God spoke to me and said, *Nancy, if you take off this raggedy old sweater...* As I was hearing Him speak I simultaneously saw Him unraveling the yarn of my sweater; my ugly torn, dirty sweater ... *I will give you a purple robe of righteousness.*

He said "IF" I would take it off. He gave me a choice, but as He spoke He was unraveling it. If I would take it off there'd be no way to put it back on. Completely unraveled; my old self would be completely undone. *Yes, Lord, I am willing.* I was yielded to what He wanted to do. His love was clothing me with the truth of who He says I am. I sobbed as I repeated His words and the vision to everyone there that night.

Oswald Chambers, author of *My Utmost for His Highest*, says God never asks you to decide for Him but to yield to Him, which is something very different (August 21). I left that night *changed*. I was going to accept once and for all the new life God promised me as a new creation in Him. Even though I had been healed in so many areas I'd not let go of the *I'm not good enough for this, I'm not good enough for Him* mindset. I've come to realize that none of us are. It's His righteousness that makes us holy, pure and pleasing to the Father. The Holy Spirit became *Someone* in me rather than *something*. He is the Spirit of God – the deposit guaranteeing I am His and He is mine. I put my trust in Him by letting go of trying. When I turned over my crusty, corrupted old life I went from rags to righteousness; *His* righteousness!

From then on I was able to look forward to Saturday night prayer meetings and Sundays again. The fellowship, messages and the worship fed my spirit. I was ready to let go of the fear that day. I began to believe He would show up and He never ever has let me down since. Fear is crippling. The enemy uses fear to kill, steal and destroy the plans God has for us. The plans never go away but our unwillingness to trust God and believe His Word and what He says can throw us off the path if we are not yielded to Him in every area of our lives. For me, pressing into Him means laying it all down not focusing on the circumstance, but rather on the Lover of my soul who is working things out for my good and for all who are called according to His purpose (Romans 8:28). His robe was placed on me that day but it takes diligence to keep it on. There are always opportunities for other misconceptions and faulty thinking to re-knit an unattractive garment for me. There always will be that challenge until I see Jesus face to face.

He is so faithful to gently bring up issues that hinder my relationship with Him. I have become aware that I struggle in my relationships with people. There's nothing like being in the company of a couple hundred people at church, some of whom I would never cross paths with otherwise and I'm commanded to love them. I've used the analogy of the church as being a rock tumbler filled with rocks; craggy, rough, imperfect rocks. The Holy Spirit is the force that moves and tumbles us, rubbing us against one another to smooth off the edges and polish us into brilliant, colorful, shining stones. I think coming face to face with those we don't immediately like forces us to face the things we don't like about ourselves. A church setting can do that sometimes. God uses the church, His people.

When new stones get thrown into the tumbler us older ones ought to just get shinier the longer we're in there. I welcome new relationships because I know God will use them to mold me. If I have a problem with someone it is often *my* perception *not* the person. God's grace extends to everyone and I am learning to extend grace to others (as well as to myself) more consistently.

22

Sign Me Up

"...for it is God who works in you to will and to act in order to fulfill his good purpose." – Philippians 2:13

Our church had an accredited Bible College on our second floor. In January of 2009 Pastor Trish, one of the teachers, was standing near a table with a signup sheet. I asked what the signups were for and she explained they were for OBI, Olympic Bible Institute, and classes were starting in February. I looked and something on the page caught my eye. There were two names written there and one was David Duncan. *Hmmm...* That was the person who last May was sitting in the church library when we peeked in. That was the person who God said, *there's your husband, Nancy.* Trish was telling me a bit about the Systematic Theology 2 course, and as she was speaking I bent down and signed up. I figured if that is who I was going to marry, I had better become his classmate and get to know him.

There were four who signed up for class. One was the fellow who had asked me out during a church service. He didn't stay in the class very long, however. I heard that his fiancé decided he had too much on his plate already so that left three of us: David, his good friend Ilene and myself.

On our first day of class I immediately noticed the fortress David created around himself with his books, notebooks and briefcase. I recall asking him a question; a very simple, non-intrusive question. He would turn to Ilene and look at her as he answered me. *Really?* And so it went. The class was fascinating and hard. I hadn't been in college since Leo was four years old. It was challenging me which I liked. However when it came to writing papers I wasn't sure what to do. I was doing five massages a day, coming home and taking care of a son, animals, house and yard and carving out time late at night to read the required material. I would drink coffee in the evening so that I could stay awake and concentrate. Fatigue and stress began to set in.

My son's friend was over one evening and in my anxiousness I asked her if she had a cigarette. She said, "Yeah, a Camel Menthol Light." After four puffs I knew I'd made a mistake. But it was too late – the damage was done. My history of asthma came back to haunt me. The day after smoking those four short drags my lungs felt awful. I had a hard time getting going, but with a full day scheduled I took some over-the-counter meds to help with the coughing. When I got home I fell into bed and could not get up the next day. It was Friday morning and I managed to call my clients and cancel their appointments.

My breathing was labored and I had never felt so sick. My

son was hovering and this is something he never did! He was worried. Saturday morning I had him take me to urgent care because I was feeling worse, not better. They took a chest x-ray and it seemed like forever before the doctor re-entered the exam room. She said I was a pretty sick gal and *was there anything I wanted to tell her*. I did not volunteer that I'd had four puffs off of a Camel Menthol Light that ignited my illness. I said, "No." Even though my x-ray did not show pneumonia my fever and other symptoms indicated that I was headed in that direction. She wrote a prescription and we were off.

Leo accompanied me into Safeway to visit the pharmacy counter. I asked if he would pick up some cat litter, too, as I was too weak to carry the 20 pound container. The fact that he was willing to be seen with me showed just how concerned he was about me. I was a sight to be seen. I hadn't bathed in a couple of days, my matted hair stuck to my head from sweating profusely and not being able to move much while in bed, plus the coughing. *I look and feel like death warmed over. Sorry, Son, and thank you...*

After the first dose of antibiotics and a long nap I began to feel better. It amazed me at how fast the meds worked. The next day I still couldn't get out of bed but I knew I was on the mend. Leo checked on me regularly. He, too, was glad when I turned the corner. The blessing that came from this experience was that I have never since craved a cigarette. Prior to this I'd have a craving about every six months. I'd visit my cousin Sueann who was a regular smoker and I could always get a smoke from her. Now the thought repulsed me. *I never want to touch one of these nasty things again.* Even the smell of it (which I used to like) was disgusting to me.

The illness hadn't helped me get any more work done for my class either. I managed to write the required papers, take the final and pass with a B. But it was hard; harder than I thought it was worth. I thought I'd get to know this David more. Wrong. I thought I'd like this David guy. Wrong. I thought he would fall in love with me instantly. Wrong! He barely said a word to me. I remember him getting told by the instructor that he used 66 footnotes in his paper and that she would like to hear a little more from him rather than other authors. *Hey, you and me both!* Boy, he was not like anyone I'd ever met. He wore a sweater with a hole in the sleeve and often forgot to shave. *So...this is my husband, God?*

When the class ended so did my interest in getting to know Mr. Right. It was early May, and as I lay on my bed staring at the ceiling I whined, *God, I know I heard what You said but You have got to talk to that man! There's no way!* My big plan was to enjoy summer, working by day and doing yard work in the evenings and on weekends. I was not going to stress myself out by taking another class. *Besides, what would be the point?* In late May I walked into the sanctuary and again there was a new class signup sheet. I looked down and saw David Duncan's name on the paper. *Oh, what the heck!* And on the paper my name went.

In class I strategically sat to the left of David. Since he hesitated to look at me when he was talking to me last time, I moved directly across from him so he wouldn't have that problem. *Ah-ha...I've got your attention now...* Again the same threesome were the only students: Ilene, David and me. Our professor, Dr. Larry John, started by asking each of us why we decided to take the class. I spoke up and said that the Lord was trying to refine me, which I felt He was and this was one way of doing so. David shared next. Before he even said anything, I noticed something I hadn't before: he had teeth! I kid you not I hadn't seen them in the previous class *at all*. This was the first time I saw him smile. Sure enough, he had a whole mouth full. There was something else that struck me: he had a new twinkle in his eye. Then he spoke.

He told us about something that happened at work. He'd recently had an episode at his desk with pain in his left arm and shortness of breath. A co-worker called 911 and he was transported to the hospital in an ambulance. He remembered thinking it was very odd that they asked *him* which hospital he wanted to go to. He didn't know which one! Then when they got him there the nurses began to cut his clothes off. He was very aware of this fact and retold this part like, "So, these woman are stripping me now..." Next tests began. Monitors were attached, blood was taken and questions were asked. Eventually he was released with a monitor he had to wear for three days and then needed to return so the monitor's results could be read. Ultimately all the tests showed no heart attack had occurred. A panic attack, yes, heart attack, no. It was also recommended he follow up with his regular doctor so he did.

23

The Switch was Flipped

"A friend loves at all times, and a brother is born for a time of adversity." – Proverbs 17:17

After feeling as though he had been struck by a MAC truck David got in to see his primary care doctor. They went over what had happened at work and the subsequent hospital visit. A heart attack was ruled out at the hospital and anxiety seemed to be the cause of his chest pain and shortness of breath. His doctor asked if he had any questions for him. David asked about migraine medication.

"You have migraines?" his doctor asked. "Yes," said David. "Anything else?" He further inquired. "Well, I was wondering if you could prescribe something for depression?" His doctor looked back through his chart and noticed David had taken something for depression ten years ago. "I see that you took an anti-depressant a few years ago. Did that seem to help?" "Yes it did," David said, "but I eventually just quit taking it." The doctor told him, "Oh, you never just quit taking it cold turkey. You have to taper off." He then prescribed the same anti-depressant along with a migraine prescription and sent him home.

When I saw David again, he had been taking the medication for about a month. His countenance was so different. It was as though a light had been turned on. The change was quite noticeable. I could see that he was still a little closed off and that was okay. Mainly I observed him. I told God that if there was to be anything more between us it would have to be David who initiated. *For now, I'm enjoying just getting to know this person.* It was as though a switch had been flipped and the light was now on.

All of us, David, Ilene and I engaged in discussion with the professor. Ilene and David had been serving in the Cleansing Ministry for several years. They were friends and later I discovered that it was a bit more than that. Ilene was like the security fence around David. Not that he needed protecting and defending, but if you wanted to get to David you'd have to go through Ilene.

She and another friend (Caron) had taken it upon themselves to brighten up his life by painting a room in his house every time he went back east to visit his mother. One time after painting the kitchen two very bright shades of blue and a light green they hung a clown-sized pair of sunglasses from the ceiling with a note that read, "Put These On." She would stay at his home, too, while he was away, enjoying the Jacuzzi tub with rocket blaster jets. During his trips at Christmas time Ilene would decorate his house. He'd come back to a bright, lovely Christmas-themed home complete with an artificial tree and lots of lights.

I began to notice the relationship that Ilene and David had built extended beyond friendship. Only in hindsight could I recognize a much closer bond than I originally understood. It was important for her to know that the woman who was to, in a sense, *replace* her was suitable for David. I know that she loved and cared for him very much. And I believe she suffered a loss, a death of that particular kind of friendship when I stepped into the picture.

Two years prior to this Ilene and I belonged to the 6:00 am prayer group where we got to know each other. I am convinced that had I never gotten to know Ilene at the prayer group there would have never been that first phone call to David. I wouldn't have gotten his number from her.

24

Special Attention

"'For I know the plans I have for you,' declares the Lord, 'plans to prosper you and not to harm you, plans to give you hope and a future.'" – Jeremiah 29:11

Towards the end of the 10-week class session I had taken a trip to Spokane over the July 4th holiday. I and two other B.A.G. ladies hit the road on a Saturday, driving six hours including up and over the Cascades to a town I had only ever passed through: Spokane. We got settled in our hotel room and ventured to the mall, of course. Really a road trip without shopping is no road trip at all. We then looked for a restaurant they'd visited on a previous trip only to find that it had closed down. We ate at another non-descript diner that had good food and big portions. We retired early so that we could continue heading east to Idaho the next morning.

After another four hour drive we arrived at our destination: Sandpoint, Idaho. The town was on a point that extended out into a river. They had a popular film festival there every fall, but this was summer and it was hot and crowded. We meandered in and out of gift shops, had lunch and headed back to Spokane. We spent one more night before we headed back home to Poulsbo Washington – the much cooler side of the mountains. It's funny, my cousin, who grew up in

Poulsbo Washington, had married and moved to Austria then returned for five years and settled in Eastern Washington. She said every time she made the drive back to my area and started the descent from the mountain pass she'd start to mold. The weather really is not *that bad*, though.

We actually sighed with relief as the temperature dropped an easy ten degrees between the mountain's summit and a nearby town called North Bend. It was the 4th of July when we got home. I headed out to my parents' house later in the day with a small arsenal purchased at the Indian reservation in Suquamish. Fireworks was a tradition. My brother, Andrew, who always spent 5 times as much on fireworks as anyone else, my mom, dad, and occasionally a niece or two and a cousin or two converged on my mom and dad's house in Allyn. We'd build a bonfire at the waters' edge and light off our mini stockpile of fireworks and sit back to admire the folks who dropped small fortunes on theirs.

This little piece of heaven on the Puget Sound, Case Inlet, would be aglow with displays surrounding it. From Grapeview to Stretch Island across the bay Disneyland-sized mortars exploded in the sky followed by our *ooohs, and aaahhhhhs* and an occasional, *well you think that's cool*? We'd answer back with our own display: a modest-sized fountain, giving it an equal or greater amount of adulation.

On the 5th of July our church hosted a church-wide BBQ. When we held an event it was usually a big to-do. Bouncy cage, dunk-tank, face painting, worship music, and lots of food. They supplied the drinks and main dish, which included hamburgers and hotdogs and everyone else brought something to share. Round tables were set up in the parking lot for seating. A long continuous row of tables was arranged so that watermelon-eating contest participants could easily be viewed as they gorged themselves on the sweet, seedless fruit.

When I arrived I saw Pastor Trish, the teacher of our first class. I stopped to chat with her. She asked how class was going. About that time David Duncan walked up and joined the conversation. A few minutes later she was gone and he and I were left standing there. I spotted a couple, Jerry and Linda, sitting at a big round table. I mumbled something like, "I'm going to see what the Peases are up to..." and headed in their direction. David was behind me and seemed to want to go where I was going. I sat down and another friend of mine sat across from me leaving a seat between the two of us. David sat down there. Conversation ensued. I noticed Jerry had a cup of coffee and I asked where he got it from. David spoke up and asked, "Would you like me to get you a cup of coffee?"

"Oh, yes please. That would be nice," I responded. Soon I

had a hot cup of coffee in front of me, compete with packets of cream and sugar. *Thank you.* In the meantime someone had handed out blue sheets to all of us. There were sayings on them that resembled certain scriptures. It was a game – you had to figure out which scripture matched the sayings on the paper. All five us, Ilene, Jerry and Linda, David and I sat there trying to figure them out. We got about half way done and I noticed the watermelon contest was about to begin so I excused myself to watch a friend of mine compete. After much cheering on and yelling, the winner was announced and I went back to the table. Looking around I'm thinking, *oh no, my blue sheet is gone!* David said to me, "Here, we can fill out mine together." So we did.

We managed to get enough right answers to win third place! When third place winners were called to collect their prize I sent David up to get it. He brought back a Cold Stone Creamery card worth ten dollars. He bent forward towards me and said, "Here this is for you." "Thanks," I said, "but I'd rather have a Starbucks." And so it began. At the end of the BBQ everyone was flooding in the side doors of the sanctuary. I was nervous because I really wasn't sure what had happened between us outside. *Should I sit by him now?* I didn't really want to. I loved worship and I wanted to worship with abandon. Having David next to me would conjure up all kinds of nervous questioning in my head. You know the kind. *What's he thinking? What's going on here? Is he actually paying attention to me?* I found a friend and sat with her. He in turn found Ilene and sat with her.

Worship was especially awesome that night but there was something brewing in me. It's hard to explain. I know I was flooded with thanksgiving. I'd just had an enjoyable weekend away with two of my closest friends and a fun time with family, true, but there was something else I can only describe as *expectation*.

We had one more week of class left. I was a little giddy for the sheer fact class was OVER! On the way down stairs and out of the building we were saying our good-byes to one another. The three of us had just spent the last 10 weeks together. I felt as though I had a better handle on who this person David was, yet there seemed to be something more to him. As soon as I got in my car and started it I had this thought, *you should have said something to David about the BBQ.* It continued to gnaw at me and became stronger the closer I got to home. When I arrived I found Ilene's phone number knowing she would have David's number since they served in the same ministry and were good friends. I called her and said that I had something I had to ask David and would she give me his number. She said this: "For you Nancy, yes," and she gave me his number.

25

Leave a Message

"For with God nothing will be impossible." – Luke 1:37

Soon after talking with Ilene, I called him. "I'm not here to take your call so please leave me a message and I'll get back to you." His answering machine answered my call. *Well, I guess I'll leave him a message and either he'll ignore me or call me.* Seriously, I had no idea what he would do. In the message I thanked him for the special attention he'd given me. Oh, but if it was just my imagination to please ignore this message, and by the way God has a plan. I hung up and hoped for the best.

He called the next night. Pretty fast turnaround. We talked for over two hours about the usual stuff. He asked me things like what I liked to do and what I liked to read. One thing we didn't discuss was the comment I left about *God having a plan.* David it turns out is a very shy person in one regard, but outgoing in other ways.

That Friday night the prayer team had a prayer event at the church. Both of us were part of the prayer ministry even though I'd never seen him at any other events in the past eight years. He served once a month during a service I normally didn't attend. I never had any interaction with him at church or while serving in this ministry. He also was involved with Cleansing Stream ministry. That is where he began to heal emotionally from *his* traumatic past. Friday night rolled around and lo and behold, there he is at the church. The overseer of the event had him lead a team of people around the first floor praying in and through the various rooms used for children's Sunday school, the nursery and the day care. I was on his team, imagine that. After prayer everyone gathered in the cafe to visit. A few friends had decided to go to the Red Apple Diner for a bite to eat. I was invited. Someone else had invited David. Next thing I know I am giving him a ride in my car to the diner.

It was so much fun. He sat next to me and was quite chatty – a side of him I had not yet witnessed. As we were leaving and saying goodbye to a couple I dearly loved, the wife had an interesting grin on her face. I heard that later she shared with our mutual friend, Sheryl, that there seemed to be *something going on between David and Nancy.* Sheryl could no longer contain the secret I had shared with her over a year ago. "That is who Nancy said God told her she was going to marry!" said Sheryl. You could have picked Dana's jaw up off the ground. "You're kidding!" She paused, "I can see it."

When I dropped David off at church where he had left his car he said he liked that place, referring to Red Apple Diner, and that we should go there again. This was his way of asking me out without actually asking me out. I didn't get it at first so he had to put it in another more direct way: "Would you like to go there again, with me?" *Oh, a date!* "Oh yeah, that would be nice," I said.

We had our first official date on July 16th, 2009. I told him that the next day I was going out to my folks' place and a bunch of family would be there and "surely you don't want to go out there." "Yes, I would," he said. "No, you don't," I said." "Yes, I do." So our second date was the very next day, July 17th. We drove to Allyn where 20 of my relatives got to meet and interrogate David...all at once...on our second date.

Every year the Austin side of our family has a reunion. July 17th was that day. My sister and her grandson come from California and my other sister and her husband come from Issaquah, Washington. My brother, his girlfriend, her two daughters, and her mother were there. This particular year a whole contingent from Virginia also came: a cousin, her husband and three grandsons. My son usually makes an appearance as well as my two nieces from my younger brother.

We converge on my parents' house which is a modest home on two lots directly across the street from the saltwater. Case

Inlet is the body of water that lies between Victor and Allyn, Washington. The land was given to my dad for a dollar. My mom's dad had bought several lots and divided them up amongst the Austin children. Trees surround the property as each Austin's plot touches the borders of another. Mom and dad built their house in 1991. They sold their townhouse in Redmond and moved in with me for about six months until it was completed. Dad planted the lawn and turned their yard into a park-like setting. Because of the many rocks in the soil and giant boulders dotting the landscape they named their place Lindsey's Rockland.

At our gathering that year David got to experience the whirlwind of conversations that all take place at once. Often times if the conversations are in close proximity of each other you can jump into one conversation, temporarily leaving your current one to add a bit of knowledge or wit to the other and then pop right back into your own. He was approached by my sister, Beth, who said, "Ah, David in the lion's den." I thought it rather funny she referred to a biblical character. My family is not known for its propriety nor its manners. I'd say we all have some and know how to use them but we don't always find them necessary, especially with each other. So date number two: David, me and the whole gosh darn family.

How do you top that? I don't know! Oh, wait…I know. How

about the next week when I was to attend an advanced level Inner Healing seminar in a town about three hours away. I didn't invite David to come, but he got it in his own head to go. The seminar was held at The Embassy Suites and it was three days and two nights of speakers, worship and intense prayer intercession. There also may be some spiritual deliverance that takes place. The Bible talks about the enemy having a plan for every believer: to kill, steal and destroy the plans God has for them. He often uses traumatic childhood events to put strongholds in place in our hearts and minds. In other words, warped ways of thinking about life, oneself, others, etc., that are contrary to what God says.

Spirits can oppress a believer in Christ but not possess. If your mind goes straight to envisioning *The Exorcist,* that is just another example of Hollywood sensationalizing and distorting truth. Sure, a Hollywood sensationalized spirit might be able to turn one's head all the way around but big deal. How does that mess up your life? A spirit of lust on the other hand, will turn your head to gaze, fantasize and commit mental adultery and wreak havoc in a marriage if it is not dealt with. Now that will *most certainly* mess up your life and God's plan for your marriage!

In the hotel restaurant where the seminar was being held at we'd eat lunch and dinner each day. He'd pick up the tab then I'd pick up the tab, he'd pick up the tab then I'd...wait!

I'm not doing this. If he wants to spend time with me I am not going to pay for it. And that is exactly what I told him when we met at Cold Stone Creamery shortly after this. He got off the ferry from Seattle and I walked over from my office in downtown Bremerton. We used the gift card we'd won at the BBQ where we first had our "what felt like a date" time together.

While eating our waffle cones filled with concoctions of coconut cream pie ice cream I told him, "David, we will probably be seeing a lot less of each other because I am no longer going to be picking up the tab some of the time. So if you want to see me you're going to have to pay for the date because I am worth it." He looked hurt, not because of what I said but he thought I was insinuating he didn't think I was worth it. "No, I will pay for our dates," he said, "because you *are* worth it." We left full and I was a little more than satisfied. I had never said anything like that before. I never believed it before. I am a child of the Most High God and I am worth it.

One day in August David was coming over for dinner. Leo was spending the night at a friend's house and would be leaving for Central Washington University the next month. He chose to major in Cultural Anthropology. A professor at Olympic College opened his eyes to the study of man. I was so happy he had found something to be passionate about.

He'd come this far and he was doing it on his own. I'd let him use some of his college money for a trip to Iceland and Sweden. He had a fascination with the Nordic culture. He loved music and he'd been discovering artists from this part of the world.

Tonight was the night I planned to reveal something to David that I dreaded. Our relationship was deepening and he needed a key piece of information about me before things go more serious. Having lived the life I did in the past it is a wonder I didn't acquire all kinds of STD's. It was 1998 when I discovered it: Genital Herpes. Even the sound of it is disgusting. The fact I was not wracked with several more—chlymidia, gonorrhea, syphilis, or even HIV—was really God's grace on my life. I never used protection during sex or took any special precautions. That would have supported the fact that I pre-planned to participate in the nefarious activity. *Oh no, never planned.* Even though it is a painful, shame-filled virus to have it actually was an impetus to finally end my on again, off again relationship with the one who passed it on to me. There always is blessing in what seems like a curse when God is involved.

Tonight was the night I was going to tell David of this condition. He would either leave skid marks as he flew out the door or not. Either way he deserved to know the truth. I explained to him what I had and that I would understand it if he did not want to continue our relationship. He instead stayed overnight. The one and only time. He slept between the sheet and the heavy furry blanket (plus the comforter) so as to stay separated while I slept next to him. He was a sweaty mess the next morning. What I came to learn later was that David sleeps hot. He is a heater to my refrigerator. He was probably so miserably hot, but so as to honor me that night he would not move out from under the covers. This man was winning my heart. I would also learn there was so much more to David than what the eye could see. He has a compelling story of his own that we hope to share one day soon.

God was right – David was my husband and I am grateful every day. We are so very different. He has multiple college degrees, I have none. He was an officer in the Army – a Colonel to be exact. I was enlisted, making it to the rank of Petty Officer 2nd Class in the Navy. He was a nuclear engineer. I am a massage therapist. There couldn't be two people more opposite than us. *But, God*...if it wasn't for God we'd never have gotten together. Again by the grace of God, I was able to walk down the aisle, in a beautiful *white* wedding dress I might add, towards my husband-to-be. Saving ourselves for each other over the course of our courtship wasn't easy but I wasn't going to let anyone come between Jesus and me again. Jesus had to come first in our relationship. Both David and I agreed on that. "But you were washed, you were sanctified, you were justified in the name of the Lord Jesus Christ and by the Spirit of God" (1 Corinthians 6:11).

It was far better than any fairy-tale – it was real life!

Epilogue

When I began to write this book it was just prior to Easter 2014. We spent Easter at my parents' house. A conversation between my cousin, Sueann, my mom and myself started and went like this.

Sueann: "I remember when Nancy was a little girl. She looked so pretty in her pink coat. Wasn't she a pretty little girl, Aunt Fran?"

Mom: *silence.*

Sueann: "Wasn't she, Aunt Fran?"

Mom: *silence.*

Me: "Say something!"

Mom: (staring down at the stove top) "I don't play favorites with any of my children."

You could have heard a pin drop. Something in me snapped. I wasn't going to accept that answer. In my mind she *had* shown favoritism toward my older brother when she allowed him to harm me. For the rest of the time we spent there I was not going along with the status quo. My sister called from California. She called every Sunday and on special occasions. She and my mom had a different relationship than my mom and I. She could talk to her as though she were speaking to a friend. There was no underlying resentment between them. Marie thought our childhood was perfect. She even said that one time when we had gotten together for our birthday's just two years before.

There are three of us girls and all of our birthdays are within two weeks of each other. Beth's is September 22, mine September 25, and Marie's October 5. Beth is ten years older and Marie five years older than me. We'd gotten together on our 45th, 50th and 55th birthdays and made a trip to Portland, Oregon, by way of Carson Hot Springs. We decided to celebrate together again in five years at a spa for our 50th, 55th and 60th birthdays in my town and that's when this next conversation took place.

Prior to leaving we were walking my dogs in the neighborhood. They began to talk about my brother and the derogatory posts he put on Facebook towards his ex-wife. They were saying how he shouldn't have been doing this because his daughters could read them, too. He was calling his ex some very insulting sexual terms. I brought up how he had been sexually inappropriate to me. Almost at the same time they both said, "I am sure mom was not aware of it." I thought this was the oddest, simultaneous response.

After our spa treatments we went to lunch. I can't remember how the conversation started but I said to Marie that perhaps she gravitated toward her ex-husband, who was emotionally and verbally abusive to her the nineteen years they were married, because of the treatment she received from

Richard. He used to torment her with songs he'd made up about her. We have a home movie that shows all five of us kids posing while someone is shooting a home movie. In it, Marie's face goes from a smile to a grimace as Richard stands behind her pinching her. Marie said to me, "My childhood was great," there was a pause, "and so was yours." At that moment, tears streamed down my face. Silently pouring down my cheeks. Emotions are not comfortable in my family unless you are laughing or angry (but not too angry). Tears, like touch, are very uncomfortable. At that moment she stood up and said, "I'm gonna have a smoke," and walked outside. Beth looked at me and said, "Are you crying, Nancy?" *Yes, yes I am.*

That Easter afternoon when my mom could not even look at me and said she did not play favorites was like a slap in the face. When you choose to ignore one child's behavior at the expense of another child, in my book you *are* playing favorites. For two weeks I didn't communicate with my mom. Through my ministry training and seminars I've learned about the 'phases of crisis' and I could tell I was in one. First phase is increased anxiety to a traumatic event. The second is if coping mechanisms fail, increased anxiety continues to rise. Third phase: anxiety continues to rise and the person feels compelled to reach out. The fourth phase is the active phase, or state of crisis where the anxiety reaches an intolerable amount. Usual evidence of being in one of the phases includes a short attention span, intense mental thought processes and anguish. (Information taken from Crisis Intervention Tips-Celebrate Recovery). I was experiencing all of the above. It was like the abuse had just occurred and my mom was ignoring it, again. I told my husband either it really happened or I am going crazy. He assured me I was not crazy.

The pressure was building inside me. The only way to release it was to confront my mom. After praying about it I picked up the phone, took a deep cleansing breath and called her. She was wondering if I was coming out that day. It was Sunday and we had been having dinner with them every Sunday up until Easter. "No, mom. No, we're not. I have to talk to you about something." I brought up the conversation we had on Easter where she said she didn't play favorites. She said she didn't remember the conversation but she knew something was wrong. I told her how it hit a nerve. I told that when I was four or five Richard was sexually inappropriate with me. Those were the words I used, *sexually inappropriate*, as these were the same words I used in the letter I sent Richard telling him I forgave him.

I didn't leave it at that. I also told her how I'd slept around with X amount of guys. She said, "Well, I didn't know." Then she said just as if it excused what had happened to me, "My brothers did the same thing to me but I didn't sleep around. I just moved on."

Her revelation should have shocked me. It didn't, but suddenly it was the secret I knew was under-girding my mom's interaction with me my whole life; why she treated me one way and my two sisters another. You know when you meet someone and something about them rubs you the wrong way, instantly? Well quite often that *something* is that very thing you despise or detest about yourself. I was a constant reminder of that part of my mother whether it registered in her conscience or not – the *part* that was the family secret.

There's no way anyone would have known this about my mom. She buried it so deep, only for it to ooze out in her criticalness of me and blind-eye toward my brother just as her mom had done toward her. Finally I said, "Actually, you moved on by dating dad at one day past 15." My dad is seven years older than my mom. She was 15 and he was 22 when they started dating. This was probably the first and only time she had told about what happened in her family. Denial is the most common method of dealing with stress. I wasn't satisfied with her admission however. I wanted something more. "I want you to say I am sorry," I said. She did.

I shared something deeply personal that day with my mom and she with me. We have never discussed it since. It was a choice and a means of survival to bury what happened to her and move forward. I can see now how her faith has sustained her. She will say in a trembling voice, which reminds me of a little girl, "The Lord has watched over me and I'm very thankful for that." My siblings and I are a result of her choice to move on and I am very grateful for that. She loves her sons *and* her daughters. She loves me as best she can and it is well with my soul.

Whether or not she knew what happened to me back then isn't important anymore. I understand my mom better and it gives me an empathy for her I didn't have before. As for my brother he is a very unique individual. He has his own struggles. I love him and I forgave him. He, after all, was just a kid himself. God's grace is sufficient and love covers a multitude of sins.

We are all sinners. Some of us have been saved by grace, the love of God and His perfect Son, Jesus Christ, who died a horrible, cruel death on the cross for you and me (and for all of us) to reconcile us to our Creator in heaven. Just one step of faith and belief in Him can open the gate to heaven while we're still here on earth. The weight of guilt and shame can be removed once and for all by Him who paid the price so we don't have to. He completely unraveled my rags and traded it for His righteousness. We can stick with our rags or choose a beautiful life. It is possible *if*, like God told me, *if* we take them off. *If* is beautiful but hard. We have hope though; hope in a resurrected life and that we will one day see Jesus face to face.

Did I fly that day as a little girl of eight, dressed in her angel costume? Matthew 18:10 says, *See that you do not look down on one of these little ones. For I tell you that their angels in heaven always see the face of my Father in heaven.*

Maybe, just maybe, my guardian angel was feeling playful that day.

Speaking

Interested in having Nancy speak at your upcoming event?

- Women's retreats
- Conferences
- Group meetings

Nancy's prayerful, honest, engaging speaking style will minister God's love to the women at your next event or meeting. For more information on Nancy's speaking availability contact her today at nancyjoan42@aol.com.

BIO

Nancy lives in the Pacific Northwest with her husband, Daniel, and they have three grown children. Nancy served eight years in the US Navy and has been a licensed Massage Practitioner for 20 years.

Serving her church community through prayer and discipleship ministry, Nancy's greatest aspiration is to become increasingly Christ-like and help others to grow in their own relationship with God.

Completely Unraveled is proudly published by:

Creative Force Press

www.CreativeForcePress.com

Do You Have a Book in You?

www.ingramcontent.com/pod-product-compliance
Lightning Source LLC
Chambersburg PA
CBHW020934090426
42736CB00010B/1138